KEEPING NYALA IN STYLE

IMPROVING A CLASSIC BOAT AND MAINTAINING HER ORIGINAL ELEGANCE

Sylvia Murphy

WATERLINE

Published by Waterline Books
an imprint of Airlife Publishing Ltd
101 Longden Rd, Shrewsbury, England

ISBN 1 85310 473 6

A Sheerstrake production.

A CIP catalogue record of this book
is available from the British Library

Photographs by Sylvia Murphy
Illustrations by David Greenland

Typeset by Servis Filmsetting Ltd, Manchester

Printed by Butler and Tanner Ltd, Frome and London.

Dedication

In October 1993 David Greenland died suddenly in Ibiza, just as this book was nearing completion.
It is dedicated to him and the memory of a brave and resourceful shipmate.

Contents

Contents

Nyala under full sail – sketched by David Greenland

Introduction

We are no experts when it comes to shipwrighting, or at least we weren't when we began to work on *Nyala*. The trouble with fitting out your own boat as an amateur is that by the time you can claim to know what you are doing the work is finished and the skills and experience you have gained may not be needed again for a long time to come.

The question must arise as to whether it mightn't be better to employ a professional to do these jobs but, cost apart, you lose a lot of the fun that way. Not that we would always have said we were having fun as we sawed and sanded timber by hand, filed metal into extraordinary shapes, or hung upside down in almost inaccessible lockers trying to drill and screw left-handed, but in retrospect we will admit that it wasn't all painful. As we go along you will see that there are some jobs we have had to leave to professionals for various reasons and I will make a brief mention of what these were.

Before we embarked on re-fitting our wooden boat my experience as a carpenter encompassed about ten years of domestic home-improvements ranging from my first efforts at putting up shelves which fell down as soon as they were used, to being able to build kitchen and alcove cupboards with doors that fitted, opened and closed, and gave good service. In between was a lot of reading, practise and determination that I could get it right if I persevered. I never went on a course or took O-level woodwork and I'm not sure that I would pass it now if I tried. Perhaps less surprisingly, I have been an accomplished seamstress ever since I was a child and I believe that the problem-solving techniques involved are common to both disciplines.

David, on the other hand, did take O-level woodwork, metalwork and mechanical drawing (and passed them all). He has gained qualifications and earned his living in various branches of mechanical and aeronautical engineering, and by my reckoning if he can repair an aircraft so that it will stay in the sky, anything he does on a boat has to be all right. We did both know how to navigate and sail but that seems almost irrelevant in the context of what follows.

There may well be other ways of going about all the jobs we have successfully completed but I'm not convinced that they would necessarily be better ways. What we have done has worked and the tools and materials we have used, which we describe as we go along, have not been particularly technical or complicated. Our main weapon has been a logical approach, working out every job step by step, and anyone who can do this can win. We hope that by writing about our fitting-out work in this way, from amateurs to amateurs, we can encourage people to take the plunge who would like to work on their own boat but may have been wondering how much they can manage on their own.

At the end is an appendix containing a collection of useful addresses we unearthed in the course of our work, and a list of what things cost. As prices change so rapidly, this must be taken as a rough guide only. It's worth noting that we managed to negotiate discounts with many local suppliers as we went along.

This book is about the way it has been for us and we hope the reader will find it enjoyable as a story in itself, as well as helpful. If it encourages you to go ahead and buy that old boat and take your dreams one step nearer to reality, good luck and have fun.

Nyala moored in the Truro River, Cornwall, winter 1989

Chapter 1
Getting Started

We needed a boat.

We needed a boat badly, for we were well advanced into that terminal stage of sea fever when the only respite is to live aboard a vessel of one's own with the freedom to sail the seven seas at will. We already owned several sailing dinghies, which is another story, but dinghies are somewhat limited when it comes to long-term cruising.

Fortunately for us this afflicted state coincided with a modest financial windfall. If things had been otherwise our plans wouldn't have been significantly different – we were too far gone for that – but we would have had to embark on mortgages and loans to buy and fit out our boat. The end result would have been the same but it would have taken longer and been more complicated. As it was, it was quite lengthy and complicated enough.

It was a combination of systematic good sense and laziness that led us to find *Nyala*. We had, like all who yearn after boats, spent many an hour wandering around marinas and boatyards discussing, hypothetically discarding, quietly lusting. We had also spent a great deal of time sailing on other people's boats, either as guests or part of charter groups. We therefore had some idea of what we wanted.

We were keen on having a wooden boat. This was partly because we are both awkward cusses and when people told us that wooden boats are only kept looking good with time-consuming hard work we said that yes, we knew it, but we thought that we could manage. We liked the way that a heavy wooden boat with a long-straight keel moves through the water without any of the uncomfortable slamming and banging that is characteristic of modern lightweights, and we liked the character and comfort of a wooden interior. We both knew how to work with wood and found satisfaction in varnishing and painting – yes, honestly. We had always felt comfortable with old houses and old furniture, so an old boat seemed to follow naturally. But we wanted something basically sound, ready to use, we weren't ready to embark on a complete re-build job. We had seen too many people spending years working on a boat and never having time to sail. What we were looking for was something sound, in wood, with a certain amount of character that could quickly be made into a comfortable, seaworthy home.

We contacted various brokers who advertised wooden boats in the yachting press and received several hundred sets of details to read.

Most of these were as optimistic and imaginative as the average house-agent's details and we had to learn to read the short-hand early on in the sifting process. 'Needs work' usually meant that the thing was almost certain not to float without major surgery; 'charming' meant that it looked good but lacked most basic facilities; 'a real classic' was generally overpriced for its size, while 'just completed circumnavigation' indicated that the boat would be sound but extremely shabby.

Interesting though it was reading all the details – and we spent several evenings doing this – our sorting process was brisk and unsentimental. We discarded those that were too small to provide us with comfortable accommodation, those that were too large for us to handle between the two of us, those with petrol engines (spark plugs and water don't mix well), and engines too small for their size (our home mooring was on the River Exe which has a six to eight knot tide). We also discarded those that were above our agreed price ceiling; boat brokers, again with a similarity to house agents, interpret pricing brackets very freely and always err on the upper side with the statement that 'you can always make an offer', and the hidden hope that you will fall for something that costs more than you intended to pay and buy it just the same.

The next group to go into the bin were those that were lying a great distance away, like the Bahamas or the Mediterranean. We didn't want to begin with a long-distance delivery job in an untried boat. Finally we temporarily put to one side all those that were more than a hundred miles from our home; we would go to south Wales or even Aberdeen if necessary but not yet. In the south-west of England there were plenty of local boats to look at first. We made firm appointments to view three of them one weekend in September, two in Plymouth and one in Salcombe.

Nyala was the second one we saw. She was standing on props in Queen Anne's Battery yard and her long keel and sturdy lines made everything else around her look silly. To our first glance she appeared to be in reasonable condition, just a little end-of-seasonish, and we introduced ourselves to the waiting owner and climbed the rickety boarding ladder. From the moment we set foot over the guard-rail we could see that she had plenty of character, it was oozing out of every plank and fitting. But we were determined not to be beguiled by superficial looks. We tried to examine her critically.

There was plenty to be critical about. The saloon was damp and musty, one side of the cockpit bulkhead was falling away with rot, the brass was a dull shade of green, the lockers we peered into were shambolic and nasty but . . .

She was fitted out below with varnished teak, and brass paraffin lamps and cooker. She had brass scuttles and a deceptive sense of space, caused by her mast being set well forward. She was clearly crying out to be cared for and we fell in love with her then and there on that dreary September afternoon.

'I think this might be the sort of thing we're looking for,' David said hesitantly, hardly daring to meet my eye.

I was enormously relieved. Suppose he hadn't liked her? I nodded casually, but not casually enough. The owner knew. He was fairly desperate to sell but he could see we were equally desperate to have her, and we didn't get away with much off the asking price.

We said nothing more at the time. We had other boats to look at and we told him so, but the process was perfunctory. In spite of *Nyala*'s neglected condition everything else seemed to be inferior by comparison.

The following week we made an offer through the broker, subject to survey, and we made an appointment to meet a surveyor on the boat a few days later. He wanted all the internal ballast moved for the survey and as the owner wasn't able to be present we had to help. There are two tons of lead pigs between the bilges and the cabin sole and we moved every one of them that day so that each plank, frame and rib could be subjected to a thorough inspection, peered at and prodded. By the time we'd finished we knew a lot about the state of *Nyala*'s bilges and had retrieved several lost toys belonging to the owner's small son.

We looked at the two suits of sails and noted that the newest hardly seemed to have been used. We asked about the keel bolts, which were iron, and the surveyor said that they looked sound enough but the way the boat was propped up there wasn't room to drop one. We told him we had read about a firm that x-rayed keel bolts and, traditional man though he was, he seemed to think that it would be a good idea to find out the facts without disturbing anything. We asked about the fastenings, which were copper, and again looked sound enough. He wasn't prepared to withdraw any without the owner being present but he suggested that we make an appointment to do that. He also strongly recommended that we see the engine running before committing ourselves.

His report arrived a few days later. It was long and thorough, pointing out things that we knew needed doing such as the replacement of the cockpit bulkhead and the doubling of some badly scarfed ribs in the forepeak that had once been cracked – we later discovered that this damage had been sustained when she was

15

rammed and sunk on her mooring on the Crouch many years previously. There were other minor details that would need our attention, including some points on the rigging and a worn rudder bearing, and the previous verbal recommendations about the engine and the fastenings were in writing. But in general, from a surveyor who was locally reputed to be 'on the hard side', it was favourable. He thought she was a good boat.

We received very efficient service from X-Ray Marine Limited. They would be in Plymouth the following week and if we would mark out the positions of the keel bolts on the outside of the keel they would only need about half an hour to do the photography and they would send us their report by return of post. So we left chalk marks on the keel in line with the bolts and made arrangements with the owner and the marina. Within ten days a report arrived telling us that most of the wrought-iron bolts were as sound as the day they been put in place. Two, the extreme fore and aft bolts, showed 1-2 mm of corrosion and we were assured that this was nothing to worry about.

Unfortunately, because the owner has retired, X-Ray Marine has now gone out of business and because of new restrictions on the use of x-ray machines nobody seems to have filled the gap. So yacht owners are back to the old choice between dropping the bolts for inspection from time to time, or keeping their fingers crossed and ignoring potential problems.

We met *Nyala*'s owner again the following Saturday. He had arranged a large bucket of water to feed the cooling-water intake so that we could hear the engine running and it sounded sweet enough to David's practised ear. No problems there. We turned to the fastenings and found that withdrawing them is easier in practice than it sounds. The rove on the inside has to be nipped off with side cutters, then the fastening hammered through with a punch until it sticks out on the outside. It can then either be completely withdrawn, or examined and hammered back, though it can never be satisfactorily re-roved and a new fastening should be put in its place. We did this to four fastenings in different parts of the hull, with the enthusiastic and interested help of the owner who had obviously never done anything like that before. Every one of them appeared to be as new as the day it had been put in place.

We were satisfied and greatly relieved. We had hardly dared to contemplate what we would feel if the boat we had fallen for should fail at the last moment. Would common sense have prevailed, or would we have negotiated a lower price and set to work to re-fasten the planks? We shudder now at the thought.

We already had the contract of sale from the broker in our

possession. Over a couple of beers in the marina bar it was signed, which allowed us four weeks to produce the money and take full possession, though in fact we did it far more quickly than that. After telling the marina about the change in ownership and paying for the next three months' storage we returned home in a warm haze of happiness, discussing our plans. It all seemed as though it would be so easy from then on.

We considered whether to have our new pride and joy put straight back into the water and sail her to our home port of Exmouth but we decided to leave her where she was for the winter. It was only a forty-minute journey by road to Plymouth and we could drive down at least one day a week to work on her and keep her aired. We would get in touch with a nearby shipwright who had been recommended to us to do the work on the rudder bearing and the ribs. We knew that, given the time, we could have mastered the necessary skills to do these things ourselves but we had enough to get on with and as we were both self-employed, time spent working on *Nyala* was going to be time not earning. The truth is that there is no such thing as a cheap boat, you either pay with your money or you pay with your time.

If we stuck to our timetable we could have the most urgent work finished by the time the spring came and we could then have her launched and bring her back home to Exmouth in more settled weather. During the summer we would sail her – perhaps we would go to the Festival of Sail at Dournenez in Brittany – and find out whether we could handle her between us and if we could live on her comfortably for several weeks at a time. Then we would be in a position to decide whether this really was to be our liveaboard boat. It all sounded so calm and sensible, so very much under control.

Before we could claim that *Nyala* was really ours there was one more formality to complete, apart from paying the money. Like all other serious cruising boats of her age, built before the days of the Small Ships Register, she is a British Registered Ship, Port of London. Together with the Bill of Sale, we received from the broker an impressive looking document and detailed instructions about changing the registration details. He also explained that it would be cheaper for us if we wanted to transfer to the Small Ships Register, but we didn't like that idea. The £47 registration fee seemed little beside what we had already paid out, and not everyone has the opportunity to own a British Registered Ship.

At last, on a wet afternoon in November, we made our first visit aboard as owners. We brewed a cup of tea on the paraffin cooker and sat very quietly, looking around with pride and awe and shivering.

We were hesitant to move things about too much, to delve into lockers (which still seemed to be full of personal junk) in case the previous owner, whose spirit still hovered about everything, should mind. It took us a while to realise that he wasn't coming back to remove any of his remaining possessions – it was up to us to sort out what had been abandoned.

Friends and family arrived with champagne and merriment, took a shuddering look around and retreated, too polite to say what they really thought. We were unperturbed by their opinions – if they didn't like *Nyala* it was obviously because they couldn't visualise her in a loved and worked-on state, as we could. Eventually they would return and be amazed (they did, and were). We sat on into the dusk and as the temperature fell we tried to warm ourselves up by lighting the old diesel stove which spluttered, smelt awful, and made condensation but little warmth. We didn't mind. We were spellbound, wrapped in our dreams, quite unable to appreciate the enormity of what we had undertaken.

The only important thing was that *Nyala* was ours, our very own, we could do what we liked with her – within reason. The obsession with seafaring had taken irrevocable hold and we still had no inkling of what was to come.

*   *   *

Nyala is a 10 metre gaff-rigged ketch and she is unique, a one-off. She was designed in 1933 by Maurice Griffiths for an American film-maker, Mr F.P. Culbert, and built by Everson's of Woodbridge for a total cost of £635. Her design was a compromise from the start because she had, in the words of an article in a 1935 *Yachting Monthly*, 'to meet some difficult requirements.' As the article was probably written by the designer, Maurice Griffiths, then also the editor of *Yachting Monthly*, it is safe to read between the lines and assume that he must have had to work pretty hard to accommodate all these requirements in one design. Mr. Culbert wanted an easily-handled shoal-draught boat, strong enough to withstand heavy weather and grounding on mud, with masts that would lower easily and not be longer than the length of the boat for travelling through the French canals. He required an engine capable of moving her at 5½ knots to be installed 'so as not to get in the way while the boat was sailing' – which makes one wonder where they usually put the engines on auxiliary cruising yachts in those days. He also needed not less than 5ft10in headroom in the saloon – one of the points that appealed to us on first sight because we are both tall people.

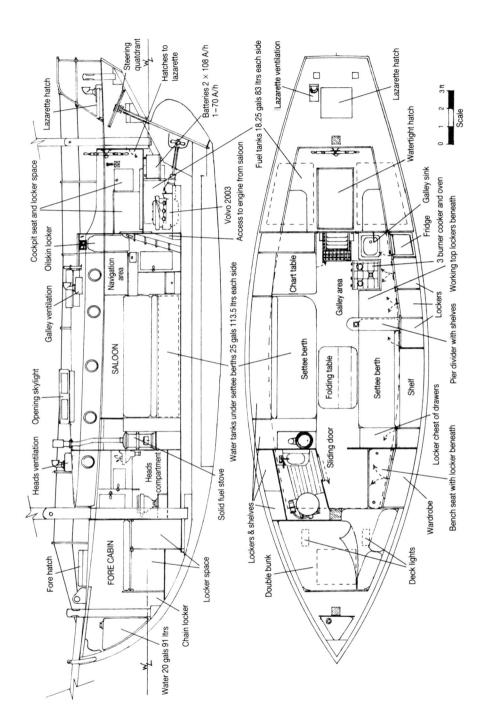

Nyala's interior layout – sketched by David Greenland

The result is a long-keeled internally-ballasted ketch, both masts pivoting on tabernacles with counterweights. The main-mast is set well forward so that it can lie comfortably in the length of the boat while still in its tabernacle. A six-foot bowsprit enables both jib and forestaysail to be carried, or a large lightweight genoa, and takes the headsails far enough forward to go a long way towards compensating for the weather-helm that would otherwise be caused by the forward position of the main-mast. This mast isn't very tall but is compensated by a jackyard topsail and a long boom which gives her a large mainsail area. She also has unusual curved ash spreaders, wide for a gaffer. There is no doubt that under sail or sitting at anchor *Nyala* is a very pretty boat and she turns heads wherever she goes.

Her long shallow keel, broad beam of just over 3 metres and buoyant cut-off counter stern are in keeping with Maurice Griffiths' design philosophy for strong, sea-worthy boats, expounded in his book *Little Ships & Shoal Waters* (reprinted Conway Maritime Press 1985). Instead of offering resistance to the waves in heavy weather she 'sidles away and avoids all the promised punishment', riding over the seas with a dry deck. This is a claim we have found to be generally true – it is something to write in the log when she takes water on deck. With frames of grown oak, steamed oak ribs and planking of long-leafed larch, she is very strong indeed and heavy too – just over 9 tons unladen last time she was on a crane. But for all her weight she has a lively turn of speed in anything of a breeze and will trickle along in light airs with all her kites flying.

It seems that her original owner only kept her for about three years, mostly cruising in the French canals. He sold her to a dentist who kept her for about ten years and then she was sold to Freddy Barnes from Burnham-on-Crouch who used her as a family cruising yacht until the late 1950's. The next owner was George Bridge and he sold her to Robert Clemison in 1972. It is said that she became rather neglected during the 60's and 70's and when her owner died in 1977 she was laid up in a field in Essex where in 1979 a New Zealand shipwright, Grant Adams, found her 'in a very sorry state'. Although she was at that time considered to be beyond economic repair, he brought her back to Everson's yard in Woodbridge and carried out an extensive re-build.

He renewed many of the main planks, recaulked the seams, made good the pine decks which he then sheathed in plywood and coated with epoxy resin – a departure from tradition but worthwhile when we hear other classic boat owners bemoaning their leaking deck seams. He stripped and completely refitted the cockpit and the interior, which he kept as near to the original plans as possible, incorporating the original coach-house, skylight and saloon table. The keel bolts, which he dropped and inspected, the same ones as we had x-rayed, were 'as good as new' and didn't need replacing. Most of his four-year ownership was taken up with the rebuild, though he and his wife did spend a summer cruising in the French canals.

In 1984 she was sold to theatre manager William Downing, then she passed quite quickly through two more owners before we bought her. We have no clue as to how she made her way from the East Coast to the West Country or why she changed hands so many times during those years, but we do know that maintenance of wooden boats was becoming either expensive or unfashionably time-consuming and *Nyala* was again reaching the stage where she needed a lot of little things doing to her if she was to be kept alive. Just how many little things we were yet to discover but she is definitely in that class of vessel which requires real enthusiasm – the ability to get as much pleasure out of hours of maintenance as out of sailing, which isn't everybody's idea of fun on the modern boating scene.

*   *   *

Once we began to get down to practicalities it soon became clear that problems were by no means a thing of the past. The first difficulty we found was with insurance. The firm who held the insurance for the previous owner was not interested in transferring it to us. They obviously hadn't much liked the sound of *Nyala* in the first place, and she only carried third-party cover. The survey report mentioning a rotten bulkhead and badly-scarfed ribs had made even that unattractive to them.

So we asked around and filled in several proposal forms which produced polite refusals to carry the risk, and finally discovered a traditional boat consultant who specialised in insurance brokerage for boats such as ours. Unlike the other brokers I spoke to on the phone, this consultant was totally helpful and reasonable. Yes, he could find us insurance while *Nyala* was in the yard, and for cruising as soon as we sent them evidence that we had done all the repairs recommended by our surveyor. 'I've got that kind of a boat myself,' he said. 'Anyone who owns a classic boat is going to take more care of it than the average yacht owner and be less likely to do damage.' He was the first person in the insurance business I'd spoken to who made me feel as though we hadn't done something totally stupid and unreasonable in buying *Nyala* and if he hadn't been at the other end of a telephone I would have hugged him on the spot.

Being practical and well-organised people, before we set to work we made a list of all the jobs we knew we must do during that winter. The list was two foolscap pages long and we haven't looked at it since the day we completed it, in fact I don't remember ever finding it again. Everyone who has ever worked on maintaining or refitting a boat will know that jobs organise themselves into their own priority and that for every job on the list at least half a dozen others emerge along the way, all equally essential. However, compiling that list did help us to organise our thoughts, and led to the stage of making policy decisions.

We realised that owning what was undoubtedly a classic boat brought a responsibility. We had to decide between our overall aim of fitting her out to our standards of comfort and safety, which would include a new heads and forepeak bunk, and several items of navigation equipment, or keeping her as near as possible to the original and sacrificing the mod cons.

But we didn't want to sail a museum piece, we wanted a safe and comfortable home. With Grant Adams' major re-build in 1979, which had undoubtedly saved her life, she had already been considerably changed and we wanted her to continue to develop as a living ship. So we decided to modernise *Nyala*, as we would an old house, in keeping with her style. Everything that had to be new we would make as near as possible to the traditional in appearance. But we would compromise if necessary.

For example, we discovered that the original upholstery had been pale green. We had already decided that we were going to replace the rather worn brown settee covers. 'We'll re-upholster her in pale green,' David said, 'That's at least one tradition we can preserve!'

'No it isn't,' I replied, trying to imagine keeping pale green looking fresh with wet oilies, engine grease, flying food and all the other possible grime of sea-going life. 'We'll have something with a rich, dark, muddly pattern.'

And so began our enslavement to our ship. We think that from the very beginning she knew exactly what she wanted of us. Imagining that we were in control of the situation was wishful thinking. As things progressed it became obvious that *Nyala* was going to make the decisions and we would follow her wishes.

Chapter 2
Getting to Work –
Fitting Bulkheads

We began our weekly sorties to Plymouth, to the dreary environment of Queen Anne's Battery marina and boatyard. This is situated in Coxside, one of the more ill-reputed suburbs of a city that has a far from savoury reputation over all, containing as it does the barracks of several assorted regiments, a naval dockyard and a civil port. The marina development was part of a plan to provide more leisure boating facilities in Plymouth Sound and to upgrade the inner-city environment.

In the little streets leading to the entrance to the yard there were a lot of what house agents call 'desirable workmen's cottages' – terraces of narrow houses that were once very basic but decent homes, then later slums, and are nowadays bought by up-and-going young professional people who use council grants to turn them into bijou residences with all mod cons. Thus many of these houses were unoccupied and in various stages of rehabilitation. They were interspersed with the premises of old-established manufacturing businesses many of which were derelict, waiting for the next stage of development. The back of the boatyard was overlooked by one of the most ugly and run-down blocks of council-owned apartments I have ever seen and we often wondered how effective the ten-foot high floodlit fence would have been if some of the occupants of those apartments had known that *Nyala* had two-and-a-half tons of lead in her bilges.

It took us some time to stop fiddling around, sorting out the contents of the lockers in an ineffectual way, putting aside things that 'might come in useful one day,' when we should just have chucked the lot in the gash bin. Then the day came when David began to take measurements in the forepeak in a determined sort of way. As well as needing to build a better compartment for the toilet, we wanted to rectify the fact that there was no direct access from the main cabin out through the forehatch – we considered that to be dangerous because a second line of escape in an emergency can save lives. It was soon obvious that we would have to change around so many of the existing fittings forward of the saloon that we might as well pull everything out and start again from scratch. That would certainly make things easier for Ron Greet, the shipwright who had promised that he would come over from nearby Turnchapel any day now to double up the ribs where the surveyor had criticised the old repair.

So I spent several visits taking to pieces bunks and lockers that seemed to have been built with the next two hundred years in mind. Because they were mostly made of hardwood I wanted to avoid unnecessary damage so that the timber could be re-used. So the brass screws, of which there were hundreds, had to be removed with some care. Some of these would respond eventually to normal pressure from a screwdriver, though this had to have a blade of the correct size for the screwhead otherwise it would do nothing other than enlarge and mangle the groove. Some screws would only begin to move after a few thumps with an impact screwdriver. Inevitably there were some that simply couldn't be shifted, or were inaccessible, and these had to be drilled out with a power drill or hacksawed through where the two pieces of wood were joined.

All this was rather nasty and to avoid it happening again in the future if we should want to make any alterations, when we put things together again every screw was first dipped in grease. Several kinds serve well for this – petroleum jelly, lanolin, tallow, beeswax – although the natural substances are reputed to be longer lasting than the mineral-oil based products.

When all this was done and David started the more encouraging business of buying wood and building the new heads compartment, I wondered what I should be getting on with next. I busied myself for as long as possible with cleaning and painting – you know, all those little jobs a woman can tackle with confidence – but in the early stages the amount of such work that could be done was severely limited. It was too cold to be outside painting the topsides and too early to do any anti-fouling and I began to feel under-occupied while David, who had been diverted from the heads and was by then struggling to convert our heating arrangements to a solid fuel stove, for which the old 'fireplace' had to be rebuilt, became more and more overworked.

The real problem was one of communication. Although we had made our list of work that needed doing, there had been no discussion as to whose skills would be best applied where, no allocation of jobs. I had quietly assumed that David, being far and away the best carpenter of the two, would tackle all the main construction jobs. David had no quibble with this concept but because we had only allowed ourselves the luxury of one day a week to travel to Plymouth and work on *Nyala*, time strode by mercilessly and before we knew where we were Christmas had come and gone.

It soon became obvious that unless I turned my attention to some of the heavier work we were going to be sitting in that boatyard for a long time.

One depressing day when my enthusiasm for anything to do with boats was at a distinctly low ebb, I looked yet again at the rotting cockpit bulkhead. Bulkheads are thwartships partitions which can be an integral part of the strength of the hull or can serve simply to divide the accommodation into different sections and to provide a rigid upright against which various pieces of 'furniture' can be built. In the case of our cockpit bulkhead, it divided the outdoors from the indoors of the boat and kept any water that might come aboard out of the accommodation. It would clearly need to be replaced before we could put to sea because, as it was, one wave on board would mash it to nothing and seriously endanger the buoyancy of the boat.

I calculated that at the rate the heads was progressing it would be early summer before David could get around to this job so I thought perhaps I should try to do something about it. On inspection, it didn't seem to be anything more difficult than cutting a few planks of wood to shape and fixing them in place with screws and bolts. I'd done much more complicated carpentry jobs at home in the past so why was I afraid of this one simply because it was on a boat? When I removed the mystique by thinking of it as a partition wall rather than a bulkhead it began to seem a whole lot less formidable.

I found myself a hammer and blunt chisel and began to rip out the rotten wood. This came away easily enough apart from the same problems with some of the screws that I had already met with in the forepeak. When I came to the varnished trims around the companionway hatch I carefully drilled out the wooden plugs over the screws and managed to unscrew and remove the trims intact, good for further use. I worked to the edge of the rotten patch and then one plank beyond, and I checked that there was no rot in any of the adjoining hull or coach-house. The problem seemed to have been caused by rainwater seeping into one of the cockpit lockers and the rot had spread rapidly because the bulkhead was pine rather than hardwood.

I knew that we already had some suitable tongue-and-groove pine in our shed at home; there was plenty of it so that if I made a bad mistake it wouldn't be a tragedy. David wisely said nothing as I began to take measurements. He knew well enough what the effect might be of a well-meant, 'Are you sure you can manage?', or even 'Do you need any help with that?' Advice would be asked for when it was needed.

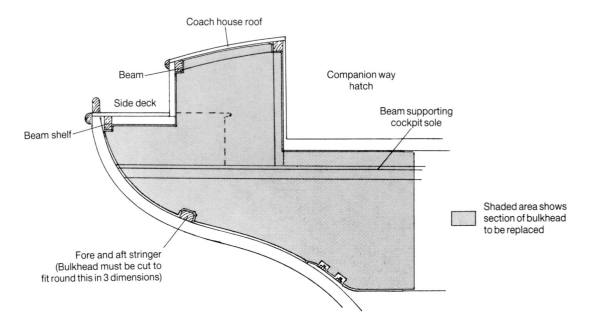

Coach house roof

Beam

Side deck

Beam shelf

Companion way
hatch

Beam supporting
cockpit sole

Shaded area shows
section of bulkhead
to be replaced

Fore and aft stringer
(Bulkhead must be cut to
fit round this in 3 dimensions)

Fig 2.1 An interesting-shaped hole – (cross-section of hull looking aft)

The measuring was something of a challenge and the learning curve was slow and painful. I was faced with an interesting-shaped hole (Fig.2.1), bounded on the inside by the oilskin-hanging locker, only 50 centimetres wide, and on the outside by a cockpit locker with a lid about 35 centimetres wide. Both these obstructions made it very difficult to reach to the bottom of the hole to do the most important part of the measuring job, calculate the curve of the hull.

The traditional method of measuring and transferring such curves is 'spiling', one of those mystical practices known only to boatbuilders who always explain it to lesser mortals in such incomprehensible terms that the knowledge of the process remains theirs alone. From the instructions I read, the process seemed to involve being able to place a piece of approximately curved wood close to the curve to be measured and as there was no way I could do this without removing more of the surrounding structures than I wanted to, I worked out an alternative method that suited the situation I was faced with: I measured up and down from a fixed horizontal, dropping the end of a steel tape measure into the inaccessible

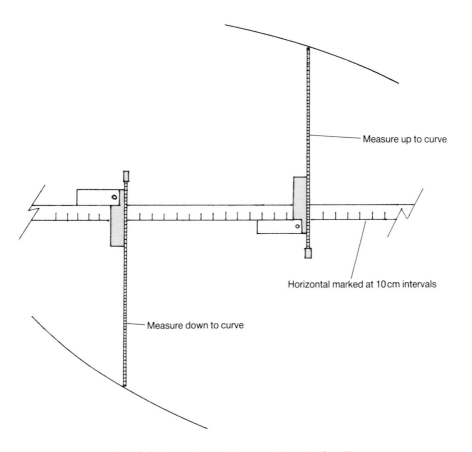

Measure up to curve

Horizontal marked at 10 cm intervals

Measure down to curve

Fig. 2.2 An alternative method of spiling

depths where the curve was lurking (Fig.2.2).

As you can see from Fig.2.1, I already had a fixed horizontal, the beam supporting the cockpit sole. If there had been no such horizontal to work from, (and there wasn't when I later made a half-height interior bulkhead to fit lockers against) I would have had to begin by clamping or tacking a temporary horizontal in place.

I marked this horizontal into 10cm intervals (this is an arbitrary length but the intervals shouldn't be too far apart) and, laying a try-square on the horizontal to guide the tape measure straight up and down (Fig.2.2), measured the distances up to the curve of the coach-house roof and down to the curve of the hull at each of the marked intervals. The curves between these intervals could be checked with a contour-gauge or a flexible batten, though I found that in the inaccessible depths against the hull it was impossible to retrieve a flexible batten without it losing the shape of the curve on the way up. A contour-gauge remained nice and rigid until I forced it into another shape. The fore-and-aft stringer shown in Fig.2.1 caused me some grief, it's probably the most difficult part of the boat's anatomy to work around and necessitated some very strange angular cuts in the bulkhead!

Remembering to allow for the possibility of the width of the horizontal having been incorporated in both sets of measurements, I was then able to mathematically reduce all the information and transfer it to graph paper which looked clever and pretty but wasn't entirely necessary. What was necessary was to draw it out full size on brown paper. On some later occasions I used hardboard or the waste ends of wallpaper rolls, though I had some funny looks from the inevitable interested spectators when I appeared to all and intents and purposes to be wallpapering the boat. This full-scale drawing could then be cut out and tacked in place in the hole to make sure it fitted before the wood was cut.

Later in my shipwrighting career I began to examine the mystique of spiling more critically and discovered that the nautical definition of the term, according to the *Oxford English Dictionary*, is 'taking the dimensions of the curve (of the hull) or the edge of a plank'. So in fact what I had done, out of necessity, was hit upon one of several reliable methods of spiling.

However, it may be helpful to explain that the most commonly described method, shown in Fig. 2.3, is to copy the shape by laying against the curve a board cut roughly to the correct contour, then marking on the board a few centimetres from the edge a curved line roughly corresponding to that of the hull. This line should then be intersected at right-angles about every 10cm with a short pencil line (the 10cm is an arbitrary measurement – the tighter the curve being transferred, the closer the lines should be).

Then the board should be laid against the hull and with fixed compass or dividers placed against the hull at the outer end of the intersecting lines, a mark should be made on each of the lines equidistant from the hull. Then these marks on the intersecting lines should be joined up into a constant curve which can either be drawn freehand or by using a flexible rule or a contour-gauge if it feels safer.

This curve can then be cut out or traced onto a piece of paper to use as a template. Alternatively, and more lengthily, the piece of

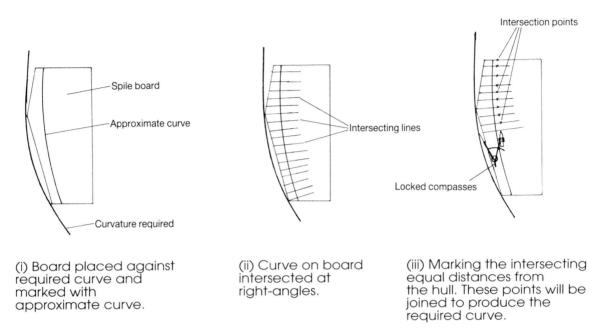

(i) Board placed against required curve and marked with approximate curve.

(ii) Curve on board intersected at right-angles.

(iii) Marking the intersecting equal distances from the hull. These points will be joined to produce the required curve.

Fig 2.3 Traditional spiling

pattern board may be laid directly on the piece of wood to be cut, weighted in place so that it won't shift during the process, and the distance from each marked point measured along the line and marked out onto the new piece of wood. Then these points must be joined by a curve and the wood cut.

Another method that I have seen an experienced shipwright use is to get an assistant to hold the pattern board against the hull, hold a pencil a little distance away from the hull with a small block of wood and simply slide this block of wood along the curve, keeping everything steady, and allowing the pencil to draw the curve straight onto the pattern board. The less experienced person will find this easier if a pencil-sized hole has been drilled in the wood block to hold the pencil steady (Fig.2.4).

Although the first of these methods is, to my mind, rather over-complicated, they are both perfectly useful when it's possible to have unrestricted access to the hull, or when making a replacement

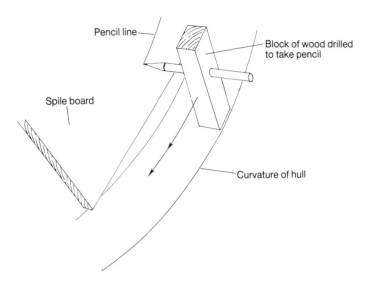

Pencil line

Block of wood drilled
to take pencil

Spile board

Curvature of hull

Fig 2.4 Freehand method of copying curve

plank, rib or frame. However, when making a bulkhead which must
have a perpendicular or a horizontal edge, or both, in a particular
relationship to the curve, they pose problems because while the
result is a nice, even curve there is no datum point from which to
measure the straight line which, at the moment of transferring the
curve, still exists somewhere out in the space where the future
doorway or furniture exists only in the shipwright's imagination.
Any mistake in the relationship between the straight edges and the
curve will obviously result in verticals and horizontals that are out
of true. Thus the method which I used, of measuring from a fixed
horizontal or vertical is the only reliable one, particularly when
cutting a complete bulkhead out of a sheet of plywood as is often
the case when fitting out a small modern cruising yacht.

Sometime during the cutting and fitting of this first bulkhead I
discovered a nasty little trick that the measuring gremlin always
has up his sleeve (apart from his favourite ones of obscuring the
numbers and moving the tape at critical moments). After a few
adjustments the paper pattern did the trick as far as fitting the hole
was concerned; however, what a thin piece of paper didn't reveal but
a thick piece of wood did, was that I also had to contend with a

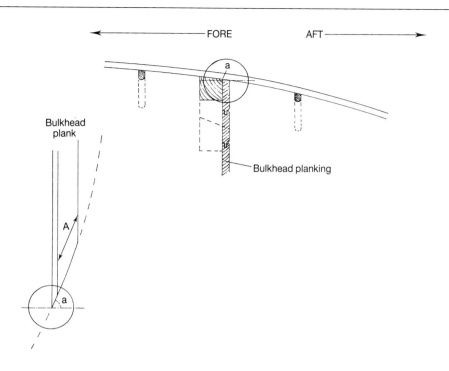

Fig 2.5 The double curvature of the hull

curve in another dimension, the lengthwise curve of the hull (Fig.2.5).

I found that I could deal with this by making the initial pattern to fit the widest edge of the bulkhead, then measuring this additional curve at each perpendicular (where I had made my original marks 10cm apart) with a sliding bevel, which is an adjustable angle gauge. This told me the correct angle to cut through the thickness of the planks. Just to add to the interest it was impossible to rely on this angle remaining constant through the whole curve of the bulkhead.

When I was confident that I had all these measurements and curves under some kind of control I cut the wood to size in the garden shed and gave it all a good coating of five-star Cuprinol wood preservative followed by a coat of wood primer. Then I turned my attention to the fixing process.

You can see from Fig.2.6 that this bulkhead had several major fixing places: the frame of the hull, the beams of the coach-house roof and the side-decking, and the cockpit sole support. These three

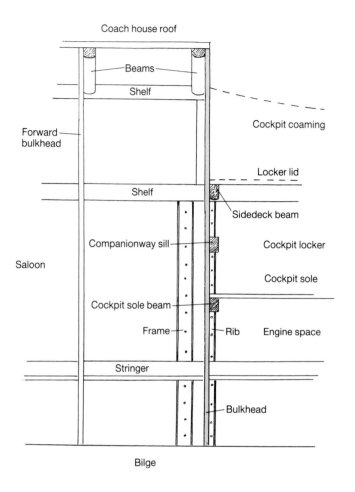

Coach house roof

Beams

Shelf

Cockpit coaming

Forward bulkhead

Locker lid

Shelf

Sidedeck beam

Companionway sill

Cockpit locker

Saloon

Cockpit sole

Cockpit sole beam

Frame   Rib   Engine space

Stringer

Bulkhead

Bilge

Fig 2.6 Side view of bulkhead showing fixing points

places were positioned both inside and outside the bulkhead. Starting from the outboard side I slotted each piece of tongue-and-groove into place in turn, making any necessary final adjustments to the shape as I went along. First I glued and screwed the top of each plank to the upper beam, under the side-decking, and then under the coach-house roof with brass screws. This was the easy part to reach. Still glueing first, at the bottom edge I used bronze grip-fast nails into the frame. Screws would have been better but it involved hanging upside down in the oily locker which, you will remember, was 50cm wide and only my left hand could reach into the depths to do the fastening. Into the cockpit-sole beam I drilled through-holes and put three coach-bolts at regular intervals, and then used more grip-fast nails on the intervening planks.

There was already an upright holding batten on the side of the coach-house roof inside the bulkhead, into which I screwed the appropriate outside plank. On the companionway side, the bulk-head had to slot into the upright of the door frame so I drilled out the wooden plugs and removed the screws so that I could lift off that part of the frame, then replaced it when the last plank was in place.

All that remained to do was to replace the outside trims on the top and side of the coach-house roof, apply several coats of paint, and stand back to admire my work. Sadly, as is the nature of bulk-heads, by the time I'd finished not very much of it was visible.

When I was replacing this bulkhead the fixing points were already decided for me but later, when making interior bulkheads, there wasn't necessarily a frame adjacent to where I wanted to fix the bulkhead, though given the choice a frame is the best place to work against because it's strong enough to take drilling and screwing. Some people screw into ribs but we try to avoid this, having found on two occasions that it has been necessary to double-up ribs after too many screw holes have been drilled into them by other people in the past. Rows of little perforations in wood work the same way as they do in paper.

The best solution we found to the problem of what to fix bulk-heads to has been to glue, against a rib or a frame, wooden backing pads of sufficient thickness to place the bulkhead where it was wanted, clamping these in place while the glue was setting (Fig.2.7). This is a job where it is appropriate to use WEST SYSTEM or SP epoxy because it is essential that the pads should be firmly fixed, not liable to drift out of place. These pads can then be drilled and screwed into with impunity.

A full-height interior bulkhead can be fitted without a convenient central horizontal because it will be strong enough fixed at the top against the coach-house roof beams and at the bottom against frames or pads, specially if it is then going to have furniture built against it which will strengthen the structure even more.

When I was building a half-height bulkhead as a furniture support a complete jointed frame was necessary, made from 50 × 50mm hardwood and glued and screwed in place (Fig.2.8). This frame didn't seem particularly strong at first sight but the bulkhead

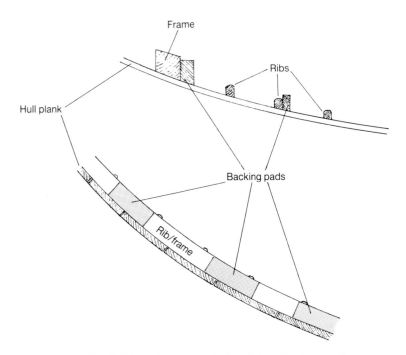

Frame

Ribs

Hull plank

Backing pads

Rib/frame

Fig 2.7 Backing pads for fixing bulkhead

and furniture fixed against it have made it immovable and as one of the things it supports is my bunk I have a vested interest in its permanence – but that comes later.

The tools I used for this first job were as follows: handsaw, tenon-saw, drill, screwdriver, hammer, spanner, tape-measure, tri-square, contour-gauge, sliding bevel gauge, pencil & paper and brown paper. I used an electric jigsaw for the pieces I could cut at home, and we invested in a rechargable cordless electric drill for when we had to work in places without electricity. As we must have made holes for several thousand screws in the past two years it has saved a lot of time, and also frustration because it is less bulky than a conventional electric drill and can be used to drill one-handed in awkward corners where a hand drill can't reach.

That first bulkhead was made easier than it might have been because I was using planks and could fit them one at a time. When we came to some of the interior bulkheads we cut them in one piece out of 9mm or 12mm exterior plywood but that turned out to have

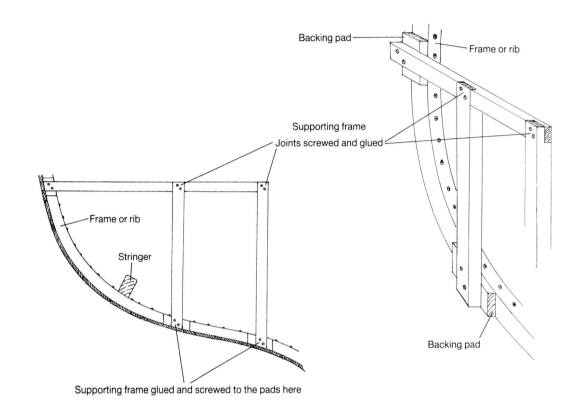

Fig 2.8 Attaching jointed frame for half-height bulkhead

two major disadvantages: firstly, it was more difficult to fit the two dimensional curves into the hull; secondly, a whole bulkhead cut out of plywood provided an interesting puzzle when it came to passing it down the companion-way opening and we later had to saw one in half to get it in.

* * *

Carried away by my success, forgetting the mashed thumbs, barked knuckles and glue in my hair, I decided that from then on I could call myself a proper amateur shipwright. I said to David, 'When you've finished the heads, I'll build the rest of the forepeak furniture if you like.'

'Are you sure?' he ventured. My suffering and cursing must have been very fresh in his mind. 'It would certainly be a help. It would give me a chance to get started on the rudder and steering gear.'

In the meantime I took advantage of an unexpected patch of early February sunshine to freeze myself half to death rubbing down and painting the topsides, confident and happy in the belief that our renovations were now well and truly under way and we would be ready to launch in the spring after all.

Interior of *Nyala's* saloon, looking aft.

Chapter 3

Warming Up – Fitting the New Stove

The first thing we did every week when we arrived in the boatyard to work on *Nyala* was light the cabin heater.

Although Plymouth is kept relatively mild for its latitude by the Gulf Stream Drift, it is so renowned for being one of the wettest places in England that its annual rainfall graph is shown in almost every school geography book to demonstrate how wet the prevailing westerly winds make the Atlantic seaboard of the United Kingdom. Even in mid-summer it's seldom a dry and cheerful place and in the middle of winter it's usually raining. While *Nyala* has a nice tight deck that lets in no water there was an inevitable problem with condensation, and a general chill which, as you can imagine, made the atmosphere far from inviting.

We began by using the ancient drip-feed diesel heater that had been installed in the forward end of the saloon. Perhaps I should say that we tried to use it because, as everyone who has mastered them knows well, these old heaters can be a little tricky. If we did finally get it going it made only a small impression on the chill and it didn't take us long to discover that it was never going to do much to reduce the damp because this type of heater produces a lot of condensation as it burns. As we intended to use *Nyala* as our permanent home, this simply wasn't good enough.

We had several different types of heating system to choose from: boat heaters can be run on paraffin, charcoal, gas, diesel, wood/coal, some with 12-volt electric fans to circulate the air. We immediately discarded the latter systems because of the power consumption but even if that hadn't mattered, the constant low-pitched hum of a fan would have put us off. As at that time we had no gas on *Nyala*, considering it too dangerous, we quickly discarded that option as well. Paraffin had its attractions, since we already had a paraffin cooker, but we were discovering that it had the same condensation problems as diesel and whereas this didn't matter for the cooker it was a different matter for a heater that would be working for long periods of time in an atmosphere that was already damp.

The only heaters that we could rely on to produce a really dry, cosy heat were the charcoal and other multi-solid fuel models. In the end our decision was heavily influenced by the fact that we had a big wood-burner in our house which we understood and knew how to drive. Another advantage in our minds was the fact that, because a solid-fuel stove would burn almost anything, including scrap wood, we would always be able to find food for it, and in an emergency we would be able to use it to boil a kettle or a saucepan.

While we were investigating all these heaters our interim solution, because we were working on board in the boatyard with electricity only a long extension lead away, was to use a small electric fan heater. This had two major disadvantages. Firstly, because we were making a lot of dust the heater would blow it around in an abandoned sort of way and then choke pathetically to indicate that it needed to be cleaned out. Secondly, it consumed quite a lot of power and the electrical contractors who had wired up the boatyard hadn't allowed for the fact that there might be several customers using high wattage devices at the same time.

It didn't take any of us long to discover that two or three electrical heaters plus more than two power tools cutting into the supply caused an embarrassing loss of current. Whenever this happened there would be a pregnant pause, then heads would slowly emerge from boats and the person with the greatest sense of guilt – the one who was least sure about not being the last one to switch on a power appliance – would take up a screwdriver, make his or her way to the junction box in the corner of the yard, open the box (with the screwdriver) and re-set the trip switch. We were supposed to call a boatyard attendant to do this but it could take some time to find one and on the fiftieth or so occasion that the hapless young apprentice had been sent over in the rain to restore the power, he showed us how to do it for ourselves.

We looked around the showrooms of suppliers of solid-fuel stoves for both domestic and boat use but their products were all rather too large for our needs. I suppose we were asking a lot to find a stove that would fit into the space that had been built for the diesel heater but that was exactly what we wanted. We had enough work to do on board already without rebuilding the 'fireplace'.

We were too naive to be suspicious when we discovered in a chandler's catalogue a round 'Arctic' stove with quoted dimensions that would neatly fit our space, and we ordered one. When it arrived we were charmed by its tubby appearance but surprised to see that it was rather larger than we had envisaged. A quick check with a tape measure confirmed our impressions – the dimensions quoted in the catalogue were for the main body of the stove at the narrowest part, ignoring the fact that there were two protruding flanges or collars, top and bottom, that extended the diameter by nearly four inches.

But it was such a pretty stove and it would do such a good job of

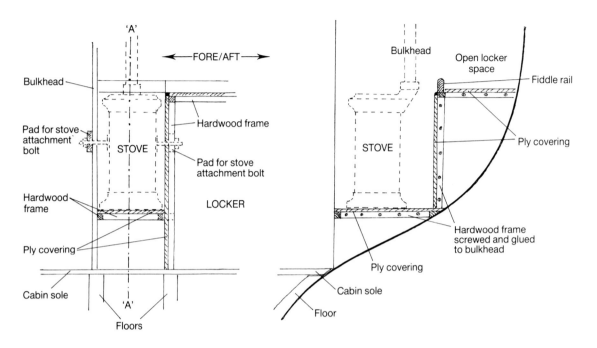

SECTION THROUGH 'A' – 'A' LOOKING FORWARD

Fig 3.1 The construction of the platform for the stove

keeping us warm that we decided to keep it and install it as quickly as we could.

This job presented us with four separate but equally important problems to solve: altering the size of the fireplace space; insulating the surrounds; fastening the stove permanently in position; installing a suitable chimney. The manufacturer of the stove hadn't seen fit to include any helpful advice or information about any of these.

Enlarging the fireplace space involved partially dismantling a locker at the head of one of the saloon bunks, narrowing it by the removal of one strip of tongue and groove plank, then re-assembling it. David had to take care not to damage the parts of the locker we wanted to keep in place but what he did was a lot quicker than if he'd decided to remove the whole locker and start again from scratch.

Because of the curve of the hull it was necessary to build a platform about 40cm above the cabin sole for the stove to sit on, between the back of the reduced locker and the forward saloon bulkhead. Fig.3.1 shows how the platform and the back upright were constructed with a 4 × 4cm jointed hardwood frame, similar to that used for building bulkheads, and 12mm plywood covering pieces. The spaces behind the stove and beneath the platform, made necessary by the curve of the hull, are useful for drying kindling and stowing the coal bucket.

Stoves of this nature become very hot and it isn't unknown for people to set fire to their boats with them. The bulkhead behind the old heater had been lined with an asbestos sheet which broke when David removed it. We certainly didn't want to use asbestos again because of the health hazard.

We could have bought replacement, non-hazardous insulation sheets from commercial heating engineers but, with an eye to *Nyala*'s elegant saloon interior, we decided to solve the problem with heavy-duty ceramic tiles of the kind used for flooring or worktops. We reasoned that if ceramics will protect a space shuttle during re-entry they'd do the job for us, and in fact they have served very well: the wood of the bulkheads has never become more than warm to the touch. However, I must mention that the stove produces so much heat that we have only once ever filled it more than half-full of fuel and that was enough to make the saloon feel like a sauna. A few inches of fuel in the bottom is quite enough to keep us warm even when it's freezing outside.

The problem that worried us most was fixing the stove in place. It's a heavy piece of equipment and the thought of it breaking loose and crashing about in a seaway, even unlit, was frightening. Our solution was a collar made of 6mm galvanised mild steel, bolted around the middle of the stove and through the bulkheads. (Fig 3.2). David made a scale drawing of this and took it to our friendly neighbourhood agricultural welder who made it up quite quickly and at a very modest cost, and it has been most successful. A lot of things have flown around the saloon on occasions but the stove has never moved.

We decided to replace the existing through-deck fitting and chimney and were able to buy from *Cruisermart* the galvanised collar, waterproof cowl and 3 × 1 metre lengths of stainless-steel flue pipe that form part of the installation kit for Blakes-Taylors paraffin stoves.

Once we'd removed the old fittings the installation was almost

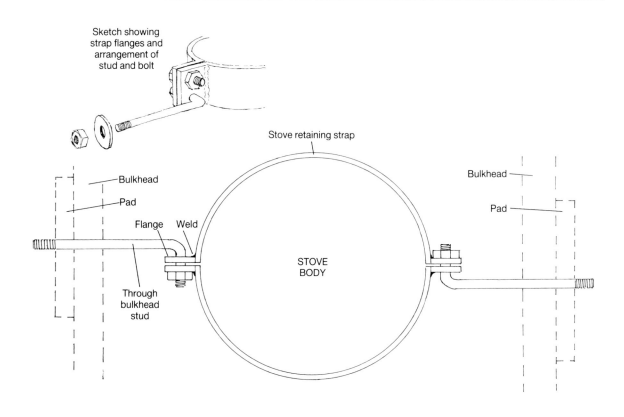

Sketch showing strap flanges and arrangement of stud and bolt

Stove retaining strap

Bulkhead

Pad

Flange   Weld

STOVE
BODY

Bulkhead

Pad

Through
bulkhead
stud

Fig 3.2 Stove retaining strap and fittings

straightforward. The through-deck fitting was bedded down in Milliput 2-part epoxy putty to keep the hole waterproof, and a circle of asbestos string to keep it fireproof. Our biggest problem was assembling the flue pipes.

The design of the chimney had to accommodate fitting over the outlet from the stove and passing through the hole in the cabin roof. Both of these holes were of different sizes and not aligned one above the other. It also needed to have a dog-leg bend in it, as all chimneys do, to ensure that the fire would draw efficiently. Because it would get very hot the joins had to be manufactured of welded stainless-steel.

This, plus the manufacture of an enlarging collar where the pipe fitted onto the stove, was obviously another job for our friendly and

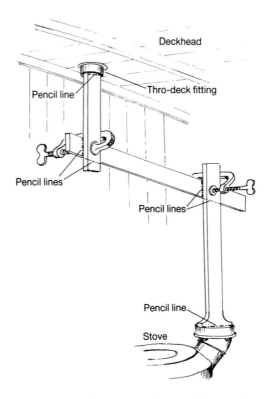

Fig 3.3 Setting up the stove-pipe chimney template

efficient welder but he needed to know the exact angles at which the pieces of pipe had to be joined. David made a flat template of the shape and cross-sectional dimensions out of plywood: he first cut strips of wood to match the diameter of the pipe and fixed these in position with cramps; then he marked the intersections and the top and bottom with pencil lines and finally fastened the template with glue (Fig 3.3). When installed, the finished chimney was bedded into place top and bottom with 'Kos' fire cement.

It's worth recording here that there came a time, much later, when one of the welds fractured in a part of Spain where nobody would admit to knowing how to weld stainless-steel. As a temporary measure David taped up the fracture with ordinary masking tape, thinking that this would have to be replaced at least once a day. It has been in place now for a whole winter season with the stove in

The new solid-fuel stove showing chimney, fixing strap and tiled fireplace.

daily use and has never shown any signs of giving way. It's amazing how often the most unlikely solutions work well.

We have burned a variety of fuels – wood, coal, coke, charcoal and various proprietary brands of smokeless fuel. All of them produce good heat but some also make a lot of smoke which is all right on an anchorage or mooring but not very friendly in a marina. The smokeless fuels are best from this point of view but also the most expensive and, apart from charcoal which is used for barbecues, not readily obtainable as one travels further south. However, together with coal, they can be burnt when damp which is an important consideration when fuel storage is on the afterdeck. Wood, on the other hand, can be found almost everywhere and it usually comes free in the form of driftwood or other people's offcuts, but has to be dry when it's used. After we'd used up the two large sacks of 'Coalite' that were on the afterdeck when we crossed the English Channel, we found the best combination was a 50-50 mixture of charcoal and well-seasoned wood. This would burn reasonably slowly, reasonably cleanly and was not too expensive.

As everyone who uses a wood-burner will know, some kinds of wood produce a lot of tar that sets hard and before long will block the chimney. There's a substance called 'Stovax' flue cleaner which can be bought from most of the shops that sell wood-burning stoves – it either comes in neat little sachets or in a tub with a measuring spoon – and it needs to be burned on the fire about once a week. It makes any tar dry and crisp and easy to remove with a brush. David can recall from his childhood that his uncle used to achieve the same result by burning dead torch batteries on the fire but we've never tried this.

We hadn't been using the stove for long before we found one major design fault – it had no internal grate: the fire sat in the bottom of the stove and, once clogged with ash, would go out. So we experimented by making a grate with an upside-down Fray Bentos pie tin, which happened to be the right diameter, cutting an air bridge in the side and punching holes in the tin bottom, now the top of the grate. This worked so well that we used it like that for months before we once again approached a welder to make us a purpose designed circular mild steel grate which stands in the bottom of the stove on 4mm legs.

Our little chimney has needed to be swept from time to time, otherwise, even with the use of 'Stovax', the narrow flue pipe becomes clogged and refuses to draw, and the saloon fills with smoke when the stove is being lit. We do this by means of two people who don't mind getting a bit dirty and a long piece of cord with a fishing weight at one end and half-way along a tampon of rag that just fits the chimney. One person goes on deck and removes the chimney cowl and drops the weight down, which eventually arrives inside the stove. At the bottom the other person retrieves the weight and draws the cord through, standing well back as the tampon and soot begin to descend. If the tampon gets stuck in the bends a bit of jiggling between top and bottom will release it and help it on its way down. The whole process takes less than ten minutes.

The installation of this stove caused David far more work than he'd bargained for and set back all the other vital work waiting to be done on *Nyala* but we didn't regret it for one moment. Once we could rely on a warm, welcoming glow down below we were able to approach the next stages of the project in a much more cheerful frame of mind.

Chapter 4
Becoming Level Headed

In a 'meanwhile back on the ranch' way, David was still struggling with his original job of reorganising *Nyala*'s sanitary arrangements. The reason we wanted to change what was already there was social rather than from any need to modernise the existing facilities. When we bought *Nyala* she already had a perfectly good pumping toilet that would even have worked once we had cleared the blocked outlet seacock. The problem was that in order to use it, it was necessary to disturb one of the crew members, fold back his or her bunk and then sit behind a barely adequate 'modesty curtain'.

We thought that while this might be all right for the occasional long weekend with good friends, a boat that is to be a permanent home must have a place for occupants and visitors to retire in privacy. So building a 'room' for the heads, complete with wash-basin and space to perform detailed ablutions, was essential.

Because the seacocks for the straightforward in-out type of pumping toilet were already in place we never considered the alternatives of a chemical toilet, holding tank, or bucket, whatever their possible advantages. In fact there is adequate space in an adjacent forepeak locker to install some kind of holding tank and there are some cruising grounds where this would have been essential. But so far I have to admit that we've been glad we didn't sacrifice this space because in four years of cruising the western seaboards of Europe we have never yet been in a harbour that provided pump-out facilities.

We did think of keeping the old toilet but repositioning it. However, with its big brass lever-type pump handle it took up a lot of space that we didn't have to spare. In itself it was a fine piece of equipment and after we'd cleaned it up we took it to a second-hand yacht parts dealer who gave us £25 for it. Then, armed with a tape-measure, we investigated all the various types of alternative equipment available and finally decided on a Brydon Standard™ (now known as the Brydon PAR). This saves space by having a vertical piston type pump controlled by a small lever and it's simple to operate, with few mechanical parts to go wrong. In four years of constant daily service we have only had one failure – of a circlip at the end of the piston.

The other important piece of equipment we wanted, where size was also a vital consideration, was a wash-basin. We were lucky to find a second-hand china basin out of a canal boat which proved to be the ideal shape and size and only cost us £2. Failing this, there would have been plenty of rather more expensive modern alternatives to choose from.

Once we had decided on the equipment, we needed to solve the problems of the layout of the compartment. This was to be tucked into a corner between foremast tabernacle, the forward end of the coach-house roof and the forward saloon bulkhead to one side of the existing doorway, which was off-centre. Of course, none of the lines between these parameters met at right angles and there was also the three-directional curve of the hull to take into consideration. We had to plan the relative positions and convenient heights of the toilet and wash-basin within the compartment, taking account of all these irregular angles and curves.

At home in our living room we practised with various combinations of positions, using books and chairs and cardboard boxes as props. If our friends and family hadn't already considered us quite mad, the sight of us gazing thoughtfully every evening at our Brydon loo, or practising different positions for our imitation of 'The Thinker' would surely have convinced them that we had flipped.

Once we had made all the important decisions the real work could begin. The job divided itself into two separate but equally important aspects, installing the plumbing and building the compartment. These organised themselves around each other with an inevitable sort of logic but are probably better described separately.

The plumbing (shown in Figs 4.1 and 4.2) consisted of an inlet and outlet pipe for the toilet, a pipe from the fresh-water supply to the flipper hand pump on the wash-basin and a drainage pipe from the basin. On the face of it this all seems quite simple – just a matter of draping the pipes around the place and making the right connections.

However, because both the inlet and outlet pipes for the toilet are situated below the waterline and it's important that the boat stays afloat, there are certain considerations involved in keeping the water out. The outlet pipe, of 45mm diameter reinforced plastic pipe, has to be led from toilet to seacock in a large curve so that it is above the waterline for part of its run. This ensures that after operation it always has an air-lock in it which prevents the water siphoning back into the toilet. However, it's also a sensible precaution to fit an anti-siphon valve (obtainable from the toilet manufacturers) at the highest point.

The positioning of the inlet pipe, 25mm diameter, isn't so critical, but if it has no portion of its run above the waterline, the only thing keeping the water out is the valve on the toilet. If this is left open by

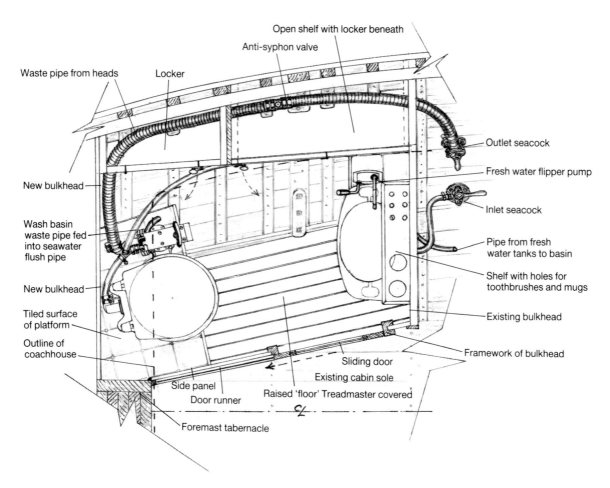

Waste pipe from heads

Locker

Anti-syphon valve

Open shelf with locker beneath

New bulkhead

Wash basin
waste pipe fed
into seawater
flush pipe

New bulkhead

Tiled surface
of platform

Outline of
coachhouse

Side panel

Door runner

Foremast tabernacle

Outlet seacock

Fresh water flipper pump

Inlet seacock

Pipe from fresh
water tanks to basin

Shelf with holes for
toothbrushes and mugs

Existing bulkhead

Framework of bulkhead

Sliding door

Existing cabin sole

Raised 'floor' Treadmaster covered

Fig 4.1 Plan view of heads compartment

mistake water seeps in.

The last line of defence on both these pipes is the seacocks
attached to the through-hull skin fittings. On some older type of
toilet installations both seacocks have to be kept permanently closed
and only opened when the toilet is in use. Even with the most up-to-
date toilets, it's a sensible precaution to close the seacocks if the
boat is to be left for more than a short period – sod's law says that if
a valve is going to fail, it will happen when nobody is aboard.

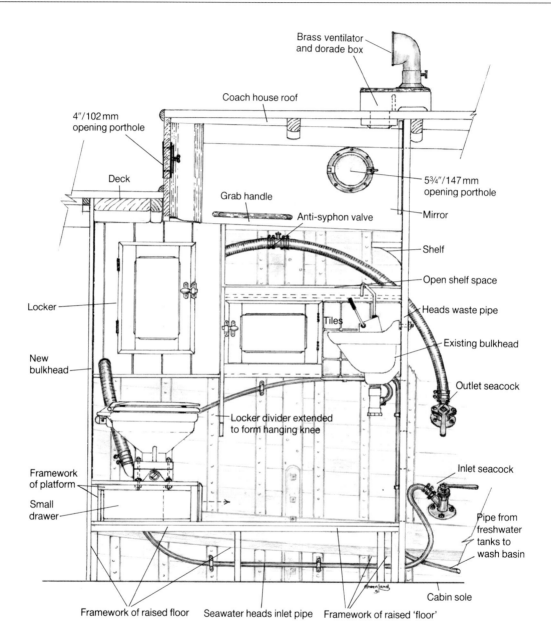

Brass ventilator
and dorade box

Coach house roof

4″/102 mm
opening porthole

Deck

5¾″/147 mm
opening porthole

Grab handle

Mirror

Anti-syphon valve

Shelf

Open shelf space

Locker

Heads waste pipe

Tiles

Existing bulkhead

New
bulkhead

Outlet seacock

Locker divider extended
to form hanging knee

Inlet seacock

Framework
of platform

Small
drawer

Pipe from
freshwater
tanks to
wash basin

Cabin sole

Framework of raised floor   Seawater heads inlet pipe   Framework of raised 'floor'

Fig 4.2 Side view of heads compartment

If a seacock should fail or fall out – a not unheard-of scenario – then the only thing that will keep the boat afloat is a wooden bung and a selection of these should always be kept on board, together with a large mallet for knocking them into place. Another potential source of disaster which has caused the near-sinking of more than a few cruising boats is the plastic piping becoming detached from the seacocks, or simply being so badly fitted that there is a constant small leak. To ensure a good fit, plastic pipe should be bought slightly smaller than the metal spigot of the seacock, then heated in boiling water and pushed over the spigot. The join should then be coated with a waterproof sealant such as Farocure No.1™ or Sikaflex 221™ and held with two stainless-steel jubilee clips at each end.

It also makes sense to fit a filter over the outside of the intake pipe because passing detritus or even small fish can be sucked in. We once had an interesting time blowing out a piece of seaweed by attaching the dinghy pump to the toilet end of the intake pipe. The dinghy pump had to be operated from above water level and the saloon table only just managed to achieve this.

The wash-basin plumbing was easy by comparison with the toilet. David inserted a T-piece into the connecting pipe between our two water tanks, beneath the cabin sole, for the pipe to lead the fresh water to the hand pump. He could have drained the wash-basin directly overboard by making a 25cm hole for a skin fitting in the hull above the waterline but below the plug-hole level. However, he likes to avoid making new holes in *Nyala* whenever possible so he arranged for the wash-basin to drain into the toilet bowl via a T-piece in the sea-water inlet pipe (shown in Fig.4.1).

The biggest problem in the design of the compartment was to achieve satisfactory floor and seating levels in relation to the curves of the hull, which continually seemed to get in the way and rob the compartment of the necessary width at critical points. Because the hull becomes narrower as it turns towards the bilge, the lower the 'floor' is put, in order to provide the necessary headroom, the narrower becomes the available piece of level floor. We solved this by building a 25cm step up from the cabin sole into the compartment which provided a 40cm wide level floor to the compartment before meeting again with the hull curve. Then, as this 40cm wasn't wide enough for the toilet unit, a further platform had to be built in one end of the compartment 15cm above the first piece of floor, which raised the toilet bowl to the best 'sitting' height and provided a base 60cm wide. This was placed at the forward end of the compartment so that the toilet, facing aft, was tucked a little way under the forward end of the coach-house roof and full standing room would

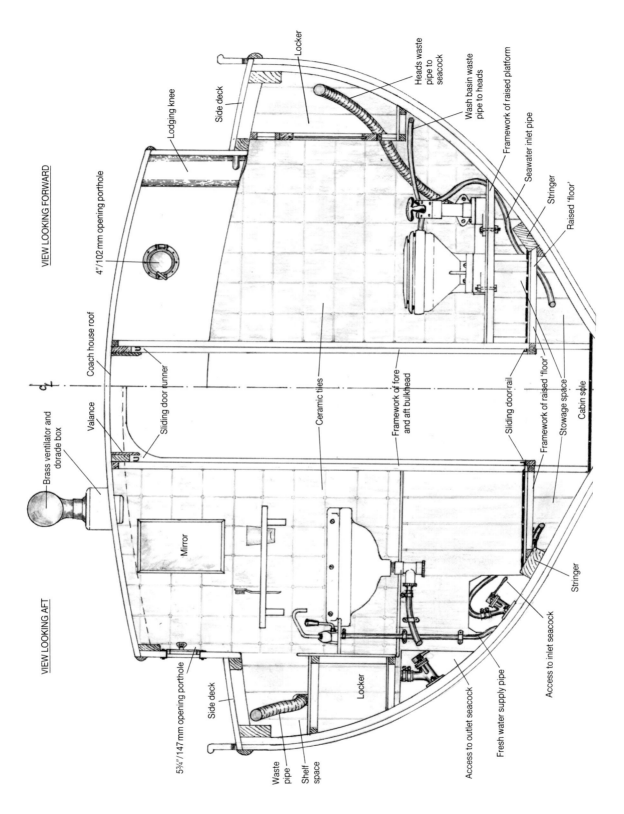

Fig 4.3 Cross-sections of heads compartment

VIEW LOOKING FORWARD

Locker

Heads waste pipe to seacock

Wash basin waste pipe to heads

Framework of raised platform

Seawater inlet pipe

Stringer

Raised 'floor'

Lodging knee

Side deck

4"/102 mm opening porthole

Coach house roof

Sliding door runner

Valance

Brass ventilator and dorade box

Ceramic tiles

Framework of fore and aft bulkhead

Sliding doorrail

Framework of raised 'floor'

Stowage space

Cabin sole

VIEW LOOKING AFT

Mirror

5¾"/147 mm opening porthole

Side deck

Waste pipe

Shelf space

Locker

Access to outlet seacock

Fresh water supply pipe

Access to inlet seacock

Stringer

be possible facing the toilet and in front of the basin at the other end of the compartment.

Figs. 4.1 – 4.3 show the arrangements that were arrived at to solve all the problems. It has to be admitted that because of all the strange shapes and angles a perfect pre-work plan was out of the question, the solutions evolved in a certain order as the work proceeded, from the inside out, within the parameters of our initial decisions.

The first stage in the building was a 12mm exterior ply bulkhead to enclose the forward end of the compartment, fitting between the mast step, the deck and the curve of the hull. The aft bulkhead, adjoining the saloon, was already in place – the same one as the stove was fixed to on the other side. Between these bulkheads, the floor levels I've just described were built up using 12mm ply on a 36mm jointed hardwood framework (Figs 4.2 and 4.3). After that the toilet and basin were bolted into place and the plumbing connected up.

In the widest section of the hull, beneath the side decking, there was space to put shelves which were constructed of plywood on a framework of small hardwood battens and fronting pieces of tongue and groove. One of these was left open with a deep fiddle to accommodate the usual bathroom bits and pieces; the other two were enclosed with custom-made doors to provide storage lockers. A small drawer was fitted into the space beneath the toilet platform.

The final piece of the compartment to go into place was the enclosing fore and aft panel with a sliding door (Fig 4.1). Like the bulkheads, this panel was 12mm ply battened with 36 × 36mm hardwood, the corners finished with quadrant trim where necessary for neatness. The door was custom-made in the same way as our locker doors but on a larger scale, fitted with a flush brass locking spring catch and hung on brass runners. An 84 × 12cm hardwood valance was fitted across the top of the runners to make a tidy finish (Fig. 4.3). We intended to put a cover over the gap underneath the side-panel but we found this under-floor space useful for storing boots and shoes and tinned goods and other such valuable items so we left it open.

Once David had finished the heavy work the job of fitting out the interior of the compartment was turned over to me. I gave it just as much attention as I would have done the furnishing of a luxury bathroom in a house. For safety, the floor was covered with non-slip Treadmaster . A grab handle, which happily doubles as a towel rail, was fixed above and to the left of the toilet. Above the basin a small wall mirror was fixed to the bulkhead. I considered this essential and I've since been surprised at the number of cruising wives we've

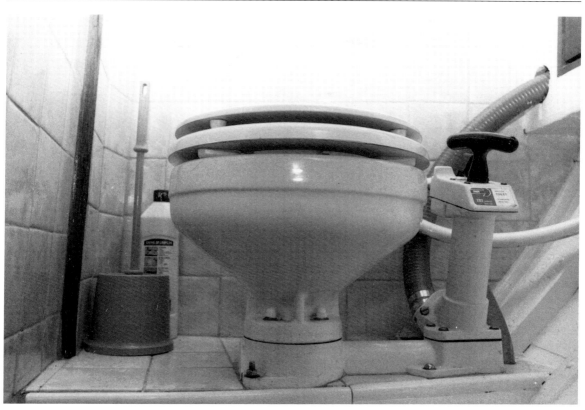

Looking forward: the Brydon loo with tiled surround

met who have looked at it longingly and said, 'Oh, if only we had a mirror on board!'

Under the mirror I made a narrow shelf with stowage holes for toothbrushes and mugs. A through-deck ventilator with a brass-cowled dorade box outside was fitted in the deckhead (Figs. 4.2 and 4.3). I didn't make the dorade box (See Chapter 9) but I did make the interior wooden fitting for the ventilator. Light was no problem as it had been necessary to incorporate two of the coach-house roof scuttles into the compartment (Figs.4.2 and 4.3) but if this hadn't been possible a small opening hatch or deck light could have been fitted in the deck.

Having had experience of some of the things that happen in the heads on a tricky passage, I wanted to make the interior surfaces as easily and hygienically wipe-clean as possible, without having to

Looking aft: wash-basin, shelf and mirror with tiled surround

resort to plastic. I decided on small ceramic wall tiles and was immediately assured from many quarters that they would soon break away as the boat 'worked'. I had a feeling this would be true but as it was such a small area to experiment with I went ahead and tiled all the flat surfaces, painting the curved surfaces with gloss paint. To my amazement, after several heavy-weather passages there is no sign of even a crack anywhere in the tiling.

A final thought is that, with only a little additional complication to the plumbing, we would just have had space to fit a shower in this compartment. But then we could also have gone to the extremes of hot water and pressurised taps which tend to waste water and cause possible electrical complications. As it is, the height of luxury for us is to lead the spray head of our solar-heated water bag in through the heads porthole and as this is a big advance on folding back the bunk and sitting behind a curtain, we are happy.

I have cheated a little here and described all this work as though it was achieved in one continuous burst of applied effort. While it is true that the main plumbing and structural work was done before we went afloat for the first time, many of the finishing jobs that didn't seem so urgent were inevitably delayed while more pressing considerations came to the fore, such as organising an efficient method of steering *Nyala.*

Chapter 5
Steering and Other Adventures

The previous owner had told us that *Nyala*'s steering was a bit stiff. 'But it's nothing to worry about,' he said, 'because she's very steady on the helm'.

We didn't comment at the time, just filed the information away. But when she was finally ours we knew we had to investigate the whole system. Not only was it a bit stiff, it squeaked and graunched painfully somewhere between the wheel and rudder. Also, remember, our surveyor had recommended that the rudder bearings were badly worn and needed to be replaced. In our minds, this all added up to something that we should be worrying about. The alternative, taking the risk of finding ourselves adrift with malfunctioning steering through lack of proper maintenance was not the way we liked to approach things.

So, quite early in our winter maintenance programme, at the same time as he was doubling the damaged ribs in the forepeak, Ron Greet took a look at our rudder bearings and shook his head. The lower rudder-post bearing was very badly worn in the shoe extending from the keel and in order to repair it the bronze rudder post would have to be machined true and a new bearing made to fit into the shoe. 'Can't do nothing about it here', he muttered. 'That's a heavy engineering job.' Then he sucked at his teeth and grinned. 'Tell you what I'll do, I'll take it all off and take it to my mate in town – he'll fix it.'

We were lucky that *Nyala* was propped far enough above the ground for the rudder to be dropped because the rudder post sticks up quite a long way into the lazarette. With what now seems to be a surprising trust we let Ron take the rudder away to his boat-yard in Turnchapel, which is a short distance from Queen Anne's Battery across the Cattewater, one of Plymouth Sound's many inlets. With half the problem solved, or so we thought, the rest was up to us.

David's first investigation into the lazarette, which had clearly been a repository of things best forgotten for many years, revealed a decaying spider's web of corroded cables and worn sheaves. The steering system was simple enough in theory: a metal tiller about 30cm long was attached to the top of the rudder post and from this cables were led through sheaves to the bottom of the steering column chain, which was controlled by a 60cm, eight-spoke wooden wheel mounted just in front of the mizzen (Fig.5.1).

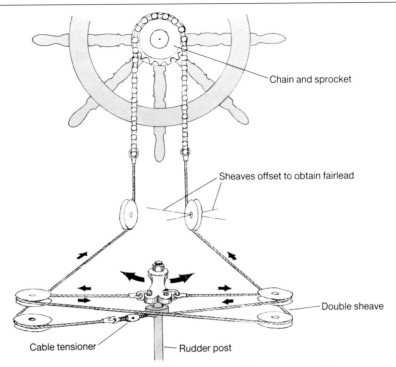

Chain and sprocket

Sheaves offset to obtain fairlead

Double sheave

Cable tensioner

Rudder post

Fig 5.1 Original steering showing cable runs and sheaves

In practice several things were very wrong. The sheave bearings were so badly worn that when the cables were tensioned sufficiently to take out the slack, the sheaves jammed solid against their blocks and the cables then ran around stationary sheaves, which produced the squeaks and groans that had alerted us. Obviously, the sheaves needed to be replaced with new ones but it would have been very difficult, if not impossible, to do this without lifting the deck because the lazarette is very steeply angled, owing to the old-fashioned shape of the overhanging counter stern, and access to it is limited to a 60 × 60cm top-hatch and two 30 × 45cm forward cockpit hatches (Fig. 5.2). The old sheaves were (and still are) tucked into the angle between the deck and the counter. David considered the possibility of fitting the old system with new sheaves in more accessible places but that was impractical because of the impossibility of achieving a fair lead.

We were also worried by the fact that the short tiller made the whole system very high-geared and thus steering would be hard

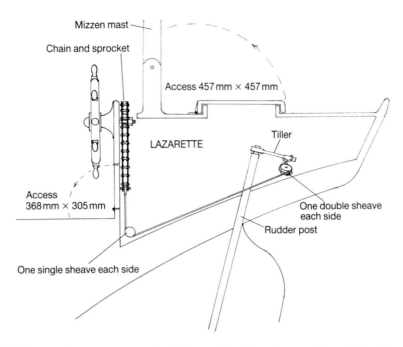

Fig 5.2 General arrangement of lazarette showing original steering gear

work for long, short-handed passages. The only solution seemed to be to scrap everything and start again – everything, that is, except for *Nyala*'s beautiful wood and brass steering wheel.

For a time we made a thorough nuisance of ourselves by examining the steering systems of as many other wheel-steered boats as we could gain access to. Then, after a long and very helpful conversation with Julian Whitlock at the London Boat Show we decided that a Whitlock quadrant could replace the tiller while retaining the same steering column and wheel. Whitlock's ran *Nyala*'s relevant vital statistics of length, beam, keel configuration and weight through their computer and recommended a 60cm quadrant which was equivalent to putting a 3 metre tiller on *Nyala* – a big increase in efficiency.

Before finalising the order we checked that we would be able to pass this quadrant through the top hatch into the lazarette and decided that it would be possible – just. The final clearance was a matter of about one centimetre which caused a few nail-biting moments.

David made sketches to familiarise himself with the leads that would be necessary for the cables from the quadrant to the steering column and bought new cables and sheaves. However, he didn't make the mistake of trying to fit anything until we had the quadrant in place and could be certain that the practice would fit the theory. Then he used string – so much more user-friendly in confined spaces than stainless-steel cable – to test all the angles and cable leads.

The most difficult part of the job was installing the new sheaves in exactly the right places. They had to tilt very precisely in two planes to achieve the necessary cross-over and had to be positioned in almost inaccessible places within the awkward confines of the lazarette. In addition, the material they were being attached to was fifty-year-old oak which makes for difficult screwing (drill the pilot holes plenty long and large enough and don't forget to grease the screws). Fortunately, David is long and lean and could insinuate himself almost completely through the small front lazarette hatches that open into the cockpit. But once he was in place he couldn't then reach out again to grab tools and materials so a certain amount of forethought and sympathetic assistance were necessary, together with the use of a pillow to protect his ribs from various unfriendly protuberances.

When everything was in place (Figs 5.3 & 5.4) the system had to

David's working position fitting the new sheaves in the lazarette

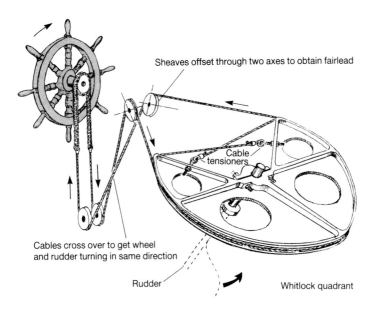

Sheaves offset through two axes to obtain fairlead

Cable tensioners

Cables cross over to get wheel
and rudder turning in same direction

Rudder

Whitlock quadrant

Fig 5.3 Whitlock quadrant, showing cable runs and sheaves

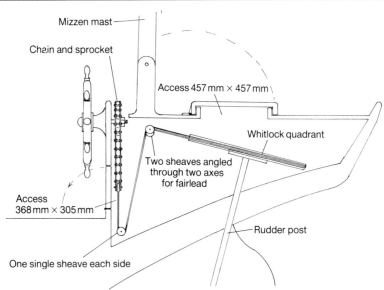

Mizzen mast

Chain and sprocket

Access 457 mm × 457 mm

Whitlock quadrant

Two sheaves angled
through two axes
for fairlead

Access
368 mm × 305 mm

One single sheave each side

Rudder post

Fig 5.4 General arrangement of lazarette with Whitlock quadrant

The new Whitlock quadrant in *Nyala*'s lazarette – not a lot of room to spare.

be tensioned by means of the screw tensioners that are integrated into the quadrant and this tensioning still has to be adjusted from time to time as part of regular maintenance.

Because it was so painful and because we had to wait some time for the delivery of our quadrant this job proceeded slowly during the early weeks of the year and there didn't seem any point in hassling Ron Greet to get the job on the rudder finished. It could all be put together at the same time, some time after Easter. There were plenty of other things to be getting on with.

After Christmas we had become vaguely aware that the proprietors of the marina were advertising an inaugural Plymouth Boat Show to take place on their premises some time in the spring but we had no idea that this would affect *Nyala* until about ten days before Easter when they sent a note to all the owners of boats in their yard to be ready to launch the following week because they wanted to erect a marquee in the yard.

We were flabbergasted. How could we possibly be ready to go into the water within a few days? We were already travelling to Plymouth almost every day by that time, sometimes spending several days at a time there, stretching out exhausted at night on what we could find of the saloon cushions between the tools and the timber. With a big effort we could finish painting the hull but there was no way the other work below the waterline could be completed, and anyway we had no rudder.

We explained this to the marina authorities who thought that it was a very strange state of affairs. They clearly weren't very well attuned to the kind of surgery that needed to be performed on elderly wooden boats. They said that if they could launch us they would tow us into a marina berth, which we could have free of charge for a week.

David contacted Ron Greet to find out exactly how much longer he would be with our rudder. He said not to worry, once we were launched he could arrange for a friend of his to give us a tow across the Cattewater and they would crane us out into their yard in Turnchapel for a few days while we fitted the rudder and the rest of the steering gear. They also agreed to make her a pair of legs so that she could be dried out upright on the sand near to our home in Exmouth. We'd have to wait until the next spring tide in ten days' time to have deep enough water to come alongside their wall but as we had a free week in the marina berth and, of course, plenty of work to do aboard, this didn't irk us unduly. If we were lifted out on the first possible day there would be time to do the necessary work and re-launch us before the spring tides dropped off again a few days later. No problem.

Some of the other occupants of the boatyard were, quite rightly, making a lot of fuss about having to move and in the end two or three boats stayed there throughout the show, pushed back into the least salubrious corner and shrouded from the general public by screens of draped plastic sheeting. We did consider joining them but didn't much like the idea of crowds of people being able to wander around our work over a bank holiday weekend. We meekly agreed to be launched, but begged their indulgence for a few more days while we finished the anti-fouling, attached a new anode and replaced the seacocks that David had taken out for servicing. Then we declared ourselves ready. The boat show had done us a favour really. If we hadn't been forced to move we might have been in Plymouth well into that first summer.

No one will be surprised to hear that launching day found us in a state of high excitement, interspersed with moments of agonising dread. This was, after all, our first 'proper' boat, going into the water for the first time. We were incredibly proud of her and of the work

Nyala being launched at Queen Anne's Battery.

we had so far completed, but we were also worried sick in case she didn't actually float.

She did, of course, although she leaked a little round the keel and the deadwoods. We told ourselves this would soon 'take-up' as the timbers swelled again in the water, and most of it did. After a week the only persistent problem was an annoying seepage around the deadwoods.

Because we were launched on a flat calm day the marina's work-boat had no problems towing us the fifty yards to the berth we had been allocated and where we spent a very eventful ten days. If any of the marina staff remember those ten days they won't think of us kindly.

For a start, during that time there was a spring gale, during which Plymouth was battered by winds of up to Force 10. This is nothing unusual for the west coast of the United Kingdom – it had happened several times already during the winter. However, the wind direction of this particular gale found the gap between the end of the newly constructed marina breakwater and the old wall of Sutton harbour with devastating accuracy and put a severe strain on the yachts moored near the ends of the pontoons. One of these was *Nyala*, of course, and with her heavy construction and high-windage gaff rig she threatened to break loose and take with her the finger pontoon she was moored to.

Fortunately for us the management were extremely worried about the sudden apparent inadequacy of their facilities to hold a boat like ours in a storm. They knew that we would be in a position to make a claim if *Nyala* was damaged, so the attendants did their best to hold her with extra mooring lines and sheer weight of bodies as she began to carve up a pontoon ahead of her with her bobstay chain. Nobody ever said a word about the two electricity boxes and a mooring bollard that were demolished by her six-foot bowsprit.

After the gale we decided that it would be a good time to lower *Nyala*'s mast in order to wire up our new wind indicator and VHF aerial. The mast is heavy but not totally solid, and it is installed on a pivot in a hefty oak tabernacle in order to make raising and lowering an easy job. We found that the lowering bit went quite well, apart from the sudden rush of the last few feet when the whole thing went out of control, fortunately without damage because we had arranged a sort of catching cradle on the afterdeck consisting of a Black and Decker Workmate with a pile of old tyres on top of it.

But once we had finished playing our complicated game with messengers up and down the hollow inside of the mast, fixed the necessary instruments to its cap and installed a white steaming light, we had to get the mast upright again. This turned out to be so difficult that we've never since attempted it without a crane. Even with the help of several of the long-suffering marina attendants it was almost impossible to lift the mast past the critical point of pivot when it could then be pulled up by the forestay. And just to add to the difficulty, bits of the very complicated rigging kept getting tangled up with equipment on deck, anchoring the mast firmly down while four strong men tried to push it upwards.

Our final crime was to try to jury-rig a steam-box to soften a 2×2cm oak batten that David wanted to bend. We got the kettle boiling on the stove then stuck a length of plastic drainpipe over the spout with the batten inside it and the outer end of the pipe protruding through the companionway hatch. Just as we were wondering whether the plastic pipe wasn't going to soften more quickly than the oak batten, we felt a rhythmic shaking and heard the pounding of several heavy feet coming towards us along the pontoon. David stuck his head out of the hatch just in time to prevent the two attendants releasing the contents of the fire-extinguisher they were carrying.

It isn't easy to be diplomatic and charming when you're explaining that no, you're not on fire, you're just steaming a piece of oak, but thank you for trying because next time we might really need you.

Everyone who worked in Queen Anne's Battery must have been more than pleased to see us depart on the afternoon when we finally managed to organise Ron Greet and his friend, Captain Honey, who brought a small launch to tow us across the Cattewater. At the time we would have postponed the trip if there hadn't been that tide to consider because the weather was atrocious. The wind wasn't as bad as it had been on past occasions but it was raining as it can only rain either in Plymouth or in some particularly ill-favoured parts of the equatorial rain forests. The only difference between the two is that in Plymouth it comes down cold.

It's difficult enough towing a boat that has steering but no propulsion; when there is propulsion but no steering the problems are compounded. Fortunately we already had some professional experience of this. The launch, about half the length of *Nyala*, was moored alongside and to the stern of her, which would give the maximum possible combination of manoeuvrability and forward propulsion. David kept *Nyala*'s engine ticking over and engaged it in short bursts of either forward or reverse to assist with the steering and in this way the whole clumsy entourage made its careful way out of Queen Anne's Battery, between the trots of fore and aft moorings that in those days were strung along the middle of the Cattewater, and alongside the Turnchapel wall, through the dense gloom of the heavy rain and gusting wind. Contrary to everyone's expectations it was all under perfect control.

Then things changed. Ron had been certain that *Nyala* wouldn't be too heavy for their crane – he said that they regularly lifted bigger boats – but his brother Brian thought otherwise. It wasn't the size that worried him but the solid weight, and the fact that it was raining and their crane was none too young and its brakes were a bit worn. But there we were, against their wall with the tide running out fast and no means of steering ourselves anywhere else. The bottom was too uneven for *Nyala* to be able to lie against the wall. She had to come out.

With a lot of shaking of heads and sucking of teeth they decided to have a go. After all, the crane would be at its greatest extension as the boat was coming clear of the water; if they dropped her then she would make a mighty splash but not be damaged, much. Tired, wet and miserable we weren't in a position to argue; we simply believed that much of the discussion was for show and that these two must know what they were doing or they wouldn't still be in business.

So, with the alarm bell constantly ringing, with the cables screaming on their wet drums and slipping down one foot for every two that were lifted, our precious boat was inched, groaning, out of the water and onto the quayside. There, still in the slings, she was propped up by baulks of timber and Ron and Brian, mighty pleased with the success of the operation declared that it was going home time.

That was true but what was home? We hadn't been to Exmouth for days and now that a centrally-heated room and a hot bath suddenly seemed very attractive, we had no means of getting there because our car was across the water at Queen Anne's Battery and the only way to get there was to walk several miles. Anyway, we wanted to be around in Turnchapel first thing in the morning to make sure that work proceeded on the rudder as quickly as possible. But it was clear that we couldn't sleep or cook on *Nyala* in that dreadful weather in a desolate boatyard with no proper toilet facilities.

Brian offered to drive us round to collect our car, then he had a better idea. 'Try the pub,' he suggested. 'The Borringdon Arms, just along the road there. They do bed and breakfast and the food's lovely. They'll look after you.'

So we packed a small grip bag with our night things and a change of clothes and, feeling and looking like refugees, trudged up the hill in the rain. It was five-to-six, not quite opening time, and we sheltered in the small porch until we heard the welcome sound of bolts being pulled back on the inside of the door. When the door swung open the landlady drew back with a gasp of amazement.

'What ever are you doing there, you poor things?' she cried. And after we'd explained she went on, 'Yes, of course we've got a room. For heaven's sake come in and get dry!'

It was only then that we realised how cold and exhausted we were. We felt as though we'd come into port after a long, stormy passage, and we hadn't even put to sea in *Nyala* yet.

It's amazing what a hot bath, a few stiff Scotches and a steaming plate of steak and kidney pie can do to restore shattered morale. By the end of evening when we crawled into dry beds we began to lose that feeling that we had made a dreadful mistake, that we would never see *Nyala* afloat again, that she would sit forever in the strops of that ancient crane on that grey quayside in the endless Plymouth rain while Ron and Brian sucked their teeth and shook their heads and made more and more improbable suggestions as to what we should do with her next.

The following morning the sun was shining and, our stomachs lined with a good English breakfast of bacon, eggs, tomatoes, toast, marmalade and tea, we told the pub landlady we thought we'd probably be back that evening and made our way down the hill to the yard. We were early but Ron and Brian were already there, sawing and planing wood for the legs. By mid-day the rudder had arrived with its newly machined fittings and within an hour it was in place and David was able to begin making the final adjustments to the steering gear.

All this frenzied activity amazed us until we discovered that *Nyala*, still occupying the strops of the crane, was blocking in a large, expensive cruiser-racer that they had promised would be in the water that week for the owner to take part in a race. They had to get us finished and out of the way or face the displeasure of a customer who was obviously far more important than we were.

The final assembly of the steering gear was trouble-free. The last problem was to fit 'stops', which prevent the rudder from going too far in either direction and thus locking, or breaking if subjected to really heavy pressure. Whitlocks had provided two stops which would have worked well in any modern boat but because of the shape of the beams in *Nyala*'s lazarette these couldn't be fitted. Brian Greet suggested wooden protuberances screwed to the deadwood on either side of the rudder, and helped David to make and position them. But these seemed very insubstantial compared to the weight of the rudder in a heavy sea and we worried about them for a whole summer. So David later made and fitted two mild-steel plates suspended above the quadrant from a deck beam, via a wooden spacer block (Fig 5.5). These work in the same way as the fittings provided by the manufacturer, stopping the quadrant rather than the rudder, but are tailor-made on a larger scale.

We were finally re-launched on the afternoon of the third day and there seemed nothing to stop us setting off immediately for Exmouth – except that *Nyala*'s sails and even the most basic navigational equipment were all in our house in Exmouth. By then our car had made it to Turnchapel, not of its own initiative but because while David was working I'd taken a bus from Turnchapel to Plymouth City Centre and another bus from the City Centre to Coxside and retrieved it.

With hindsight, knowing what happened next, we would have

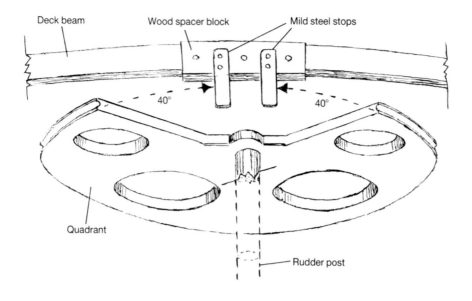

Fig 5.5 The rudder stops

been better off if we'd ignored the lack of sails, chart, compass, VHF radio, dinghy, sea trials and all the other niceties of safety and common sense and motored out of Plymouth Sound then and there, on through the night to Exmouth. We could have done it, we knew that stretch of coast well enough. But we accepted the loan of one of the Greet's moorings in the Cattewater and the use of a leaky little tender and drove back to Exmouth to collect everything we would need. We planned to spend the Easter weekend – the weekend of the fateful boat show at Queen Anne's Battery – bending on the sails, trying *Nyala* out in Plymouth Sound, then sailing her back to Exmouth.

'We'll be back by Monday evening,' we told our friends and neighbours in Exmouth. 'Keep a look-out for us coming up the channel.'

We should have known better, shouldn't we?

Chapter 6
Taking Nyala *Home*

The cool grey dawn was just starting to lighten the sky when we slipped the mooring in Turnchapel and began our first voyage in *Nyala* that Easter Monday morning. With our non-standard paraffin navigation lights glowing comfortably as they must have done for a dozen owners over the years, we trickled past RAF Mountbatten, across Jennycliff Bay and past Fort Bovisand and the eastern end of Plymouth Breakwater.

We'd returned to Plymouth on the Saturday with a loaded car: sails, warps, fenders, cans of fuel, our new Tinker Traveller inflatable tender-cum-liferaft with oars and our old Seagull engine and, with a great deal of foresight, enough food for several days. *Nyala* looked really pretty sitting on the mooring. Once her broad bilge was hidden below the water she looked less like a rhinoceros and more like the graceful antelope she was named after, though why anybody should name a British yacht after an East African antelope has often puzzled us.

The new Tinker, which had so impressed us at the London Boat Show earlier in the year that we'd decided to make it one of our departures from tradition, had its first chance to demonstrate its amazing stability and load-carrying capacity as we piled it high with our equipment and buzzed across the water, moving everything on board with only two trips back and forth where a more conventional tender would have needed twice as many. We left our car locked in a small car park near Greet's boatyard with a promise that we would return for it within a couple of days

The next day, a beautiful sunny spring Sunday, we worked to prepare *Nyala* for the trip. My main job was bending on sails and experimenting to find out exactly how the things went up and down with the complicated gaff rigging. David was busy fuelling the engine and checking it out just in case we weren't able to sail all the way back to Exmouth. Contrary to our optimistic expectations these jobs took us all day so we had to miss out the planned afternoon sail in Plymouth Sound. Come evening we deflated the Tinker and lashed it on deck, cleared the chart table and generally made ready for a pre-dawn departure so that we could be sure of reaching the mouth of the River Exe, 50 nautical miles away, on a flood tide and just before dark.

Once past the breakwater we made sail and just managed to lay the correct course to windward into the light easterly that had been forecast the previous evening. Only as we came out of the shelter of the cliffs to cross Wembury Bay did we realise that it wasn't so light, probably nearing a Force 5, and *Nyala* was heeling and romping along under main and two working headsails.

'I don't think we need the mizzen,' David said. 'We'll be home by mid-afternoon if it keeps on like this.'

Then the VHF radio began to crackle and we heard the familiar calm and collected tones of the Brixham Coastguard offering all ships a navigation warning on Channel 67. Dutifully we tuned in to hear that the weather forecast had been modified to easterly Force 6, possibly 7, and the sea in Torbay was already 'very rough'.

'Strange,' David commented. 'They don't usually exaggerate.'

I agreed. They usually erred in the other direction, or at least conditions always seemed to be worse than they reported. We had no thought of changing our plans but we were a little concerned: Torbay is wide open to the east and we had to cross it to reach Exmouth. We knew that easterly winds in the English Channel are almost invariably the result of high pressure building over England squeezing up against a depression held stationary over France because of continental high pressure to the East. These easterlies can escalate suddenly, funnelling down the Channel and building nasty seas around the headlands especially on east-going tidal streams. They can also last for more than a week at a time, until the low pressure area fills and stabilises.

With that knowledge, coupled with the Coastguards' warning, it would have made a lot of sense to turn around and go back to Plymouth. But, apart from the feeling of disappointment, we knew that a delay would set back all our plans to spend a couple of months working on her in the mud berth at the bottom of our garden in Exmouth so that we could have her ready in time to make the crossing to France, to the gathering of traditional boats at Douarnenez in early August.

Anyway, we thought that if we couldn't handle a little easterly gale in the English Channel we had no business thinking we were going to sail *Nyala*, or any other small boat, around the world. So we pulled down a reef in the mainsail and carried on.

It was fine, spirited sailing for the next few hours, across Wembury and Bigbury Bays, past Bolt Tail and Bolt Head and the entrance to Salcombe Harbour. It was only when we rounded Prawle Point, the most southerly extremity in our path, that we came into the full influence of the easterly wind and the short, steep seas it was kicking up.

Our first voyage in *Nyala*, David in foreground.
(Note the plastic carrier bag over the saloon ventilator hole).

At Prawle we had to change onto a course slightly north of east to reach Start Point, four nautical miles further on. Past Start the land falls away sharply to the north, causing the headland to be a vicious tidal race with overfalls and eddies, and it is invariably a no-go area when the tide is against your direction of passage. Thus we had planned our progress carefully so that we would arrive at Start soon after the beginning of the east-going tidal stream, which of course meant that the five knot tide was flowing into the teeth of the near-gale causing a very rough, irregular sea.

We shrugged and pressed on. We could just keep the sails filled and David started the engine to help us along.

The murky visibility that is always associated with an easterly gale in those parts had begun to close in and all we could see of the land not a mile distant was a grey blur broken by the white finger of the Start Point lighthouse. Usually this lighthouse would slide quickly by as the tide spilled us into Start Bay. Today it seemed to remain stationary.

David decided that we weren't going to clear the headland on the tack we were on and just as we were preparing to alter course onto the opposite tack a small coaster loomed out of the murk behind us and passed perilously close as it overtook us. We weren't surprised that it hadn't seen us but we should have spotted it sooner. If we'd tacked a few minutes earlier we would have put ourselves right in its path. We decided to stick close to the coast, out of the way of further traffic, and the only way we could do that was to lower the sails and carry on with just the engine.

Then we had our first experience of battling with *Nyala*'s gaff boom and enormous mainsail, to say nothing of two lively headsails, one of them with a Wykham-Martin roller furling gear that would neither wind up nor come down easily in those conditions. Luckily, we immediately hit on the only safe way of controlling the main gaff – or was it that we'd read about it somewhere and unconsciously absorbed the lesson? Without actually making the mistake of letting go of the halyards, we loosened the twin topping lifts and let the whole thing, boom, sail and gaff, run as quickly as possible onto the deck. There with the two booms at rest instead of thrashing around threatening to sweep us overboard, we had only to deal with billowing canvas, and it was so wet by that time that it floundered rather than billowed.

As we flopped exhausted into the cockpit we stole a look across the water at Start Point lighthouse and saw that it was still in the same place as it had been half an hour ago, even though *Nyala* was now motoring flat out. We were very quickly learning about the high windage factor of the top-hamper of a gaff rig. Faced with a gale and steep seas, *Nyala* simply could do little more than hold her position. She was perilously under-engined for her weight. What if the tide had been against us as well?

Then a buzzer sounded and a red light flashed on the instrument panel. The engine was overheating. Why? David had checked everything out the previous day.

He left me on the helm and made a brief inspection from the saloon engine hatch. Looking up a few moments later with a worried face he said 'I think we're rolling so much that the cooling water intake is only able to take water half the time. And there's a lot of diesel fuel in the bilge. I don't like the look of it. We can't go on like this for long.'

'There's a lot of water swishing around down there'

'Yes. I wasn't going to mention it but the electric bilge pump was blocked. I've cleared it but the bilge is full of sawdust and shavings and it'll probably happen again in a few minutes.'

I don't think either of us panicked but we did wonder whether we were going to get to test our Tinker as a life-raft sooner than expected and what it would be like tossing about in those seas. David suggested that we turn tail and go to Salcombe. We had passed it hours ago but in fact it was only a few miles back. It's a harbour with a slightly tricky entrance but fairly sheltered from the east, and we knew it well.

I find it hard to believe now, but because I so much hate turning back I was against this plan and still wanted to press on and try at least to make Dartmouth. 'We'll be stuck in Salcombe for days,' I complained, 'and we'll miss the spring tide at Exmouth.'

But common sense quickly prevailed. We were tired, we had engine problems and bilge pump problems and were trying to head into a rising gale with poor visibility. To try to carry on would have been sheer stupidity.

David put the helm over. Very slowly *Nyala* lumbered round until we were on our new course to clear Prawle Point before we reached the shelter of Salcombe Range. As if a magic wand had been waved, everything became easier – the motion, the weather, the way *Nyala* dealt with the seas – yet the only thing that had changed was our direction relative to it all. Where had we read that a well-built gaffer will go anywhere as long as you don't try to make her go where she doesn't want to?

'Let's try a sail,' suggested David. 'Just a little one, to give the engine a rest.'

He put up the mizzen and I went forward and hoisted one headsail and we were able to turn off the engine altogether. With thirty-three knots of wind behind her, *Nyala* simply flew. It's about six nautical miles from Start Point to Salcombe Bar and we covered it in forty-five minutes, then had to spend a further twenty hanging around outside the notorious bar until the tide was high enough to cross it safely. Once inside we were met by the friendly harbourmaster who led us to a quiet mooring alongside a pontoon in the part of the harbour known as 'The Bag'. We lit our stove and dried out, listening to the wind screaming over the tops of the surrounding hills and, a little guiltily, wrapping ourselves around the bottle of Scotch we had brought with us to celebrate our arrival in Exmouth.

We were trapped in Salcombe for over a week. Geographically we needn't have been because it's only a few miles to either Plymouth, where we could have collected our car, or Exmouth where we could have collected ourselves. But Salcombe is a town mercifully blessed with so little in the way of public transport facilities that it's easier not to even start thinking of going anywhere without a car. It took all our spare energy the following day to even get ashore to a telephone to let our family know that we were safe.

Salcombe is also blessed by being the home of the Island Cruising Club, a friendly sailing organisation of which we are members and where we had learnt a lot of our seamanship skills. Across the pontoon from us was moored *Hoshi*, the eighty-year-old schooner that is the club's flagship, undergoing her spring re-fit. So, resigned to not being able to go anywhere for several days, we unpacked our tools and carried on with our work in the company of old friends.

* * *

After our experience of trying to work on deck while *Nyala* was being tossed and rolled by rough seas, I decided that my next task must be to fit permanent safety lines along the deck and strong points in the cockpit to clip our harnesses to (Fig.6.1). We'd already thought about this and bought the necessary number of U-bolts and even gone so far as to measure the distance along the side-decking and get eyes spliced in either end of two pieces of rigging wire that were more than strong enough to hold the weight of a human body stopping at high speed. All that had been lacking was time to complete the job.

Fitting a U-bolt doesn't sound difficult. Two holes of the correct diameter have to be drilled through the deck or bulkhead the correct distance apart, the bolt passed through with the outer stop already in place, then the inner stop fitted and the nuts, with washers, tightened against it. To ensure a watertight seal the outer stop of the bolt should be bedded in putty. To add strength to the deck where the bolt is fixed, to prevent the bolt just being yanked out with the grain when under strain, a backing pad should be fixed on the inside made either of good quality plywood or of hardwood with the grain going in the opposite way to the grain of the top wood (Fig. 6.2). In the case of fixing these bolts to a fibreglass deck or bulkhead, the backing pad should ideally be extended to some other convenient strong point such as a beam.

In practice problems can arise if either or both of the holes for the two ends of the bolt are not drilled accurately at right angles through the deck. Trying to force the bolt through two diverging holes is difficult and, if it is achieved, the two ends of the bolt will be

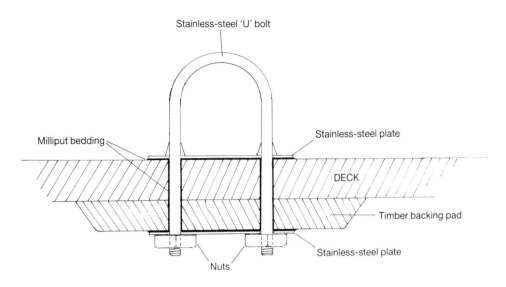

Fig 6.1 Stainless-steel 'U' bolt fitted through deck

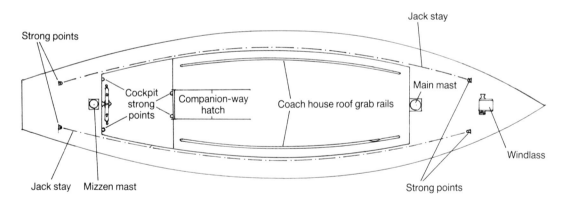

Fig 6.2 Deck plan showing strong points for safety harness

further apart from each other on the inside than the outside. Then the backing pad has to be put in place over these two ends which are now not the same distance apart as they were when the measurements we taken for drilling the holes in the pad. As both the wood of the pad and the stainless steel of the bolt are flexible to some degree, this might be managed with the help of a couple of sharp blows with a hammer. But then, unfortunately the last part of the job is to fit the inner stop over the two ends of the bolt and I'm afraid there is no way this will go if the distance between them has been altered.

There is nothing for it but to make sure the drill goes through in the first place at the correct angle every time, by checking the alignment of the drill through both vertical planes with a tri-square.

I struggled with all this, learning the hard way, and it took me two days to fix four strong points in the cockpit and four on the deck for the jack-stay safety line. When I was fitting the bolts for the safety line I spaced them about six inches wider apart than the length of the lines, checking before drilling that I was clear of any deck beams below. The lines were then shackled on at one end and lashed with plaited cord at the other, which allowed for adjustment if necessary and for them to be cut free if necessary in an emergency. The last part of the job was to 'mouse' – i.e. lock – the pins of the shackles with monel wire to prevent them working loose and pitching one of us into the sea one dark night.

While I was busy with all this, David decided to spend his time trying to track down the source of the persistent leak in *Nyala's* deadwoods which, after three weeks afloat, should have 'taken-up' but hadn't. I began to grow used to the sight of his backside as he poked and peered around in the nether regions of the bilges with the aid of a spike and a torch to find out where the water was coming in. The previous owner had vaguely said something about a leaking stern gland that needed repacking and of course David trustingly assumed that this must be the cause of the problem. It wasn't. Patiently, step by step, *Nyala* led him to the source of the trouble and showed him what he should do about it.

In fact the leak had not one source but three, two of them due to careless maintenance in the past and potentially quite serious. At some time a larger propeller had been fitted than *Nyala* was designed for and in order to make room for it a wedge had been chopped out of the deadwoods, slicing off the head of the large copper bolt that secured the deadwoods together. Water was seeping up through the bolt hole and then through some of the joins between the deadwood timbers and it seemed likely that the timbers themselves might be starting to work loose.

The second problem was where several planks on the port side had, at some time, been refitted to the deadwood with brass screws rather than proper fastenings which would have meant removing the engine to get to the inside end of the fastenings. These brass screws had lost their zinc content and disintegrated, as brass will when immersed in salt water, which is why brass should never be used below the waterline. As a result, much of *Nyala*'s backside was like a sieve.

The third problem was due to rusting and cracking in the stainless-steel exhaust water-lock box deep in the bilges, allowing warm oily water to invade the bilges when the engine was running.

Although David discovered the worst while we were afloat in Salcombe none of these problems could be solved until we had *Nyala* high and dry in Exmouth. Putting a new bolt in the deadwoods was potentially quite simple, though it could only be done after removing most of the steering gear he had so laboriously put in place. The brass screws were initially replaced with larger ones set on a mixture of putty and red lead but later, when the engine was being changed, the fastenings were replaced properly with copper nails and roves.

David tried to replace the water-lock box with a new, modern one, but simply could not find one to fit the space available. It was impossible to repair the existing box, which had obviously been tailor-made to fit the turn of *Nyala*'s bilge, so David encased it in the two-part 'Rust Hole Filler' made by Plastic Padding Limited, which worked very well until he had an opportunity to have a replacement made by a specialist stainless-steel welder.

There were, of course, other jobs that got done during that peaceful week in Salcombe. There was time to wire and fix the complete system of electric navigation lights that we had bought to replace the paraffin ones which were quaint but inconvenient, and non-standard according to Department of Trade regulations. The new 'Aqua Signal'™ lights we had bought – stern, masthead, port and starboard (*Nyala* already had a tri-colour for sailing) are guaranteed to conform to these regulations, which govern the brightness of light for the size of boat and therefore how far away one can be seen. There are people who don't consider this very important and even recommend saving money by making lights out of coffee jars, but it seems to us that small boats already run enough risk of not being seen without the extra hazard of showing inadequate lights.

Still on the subject of being visible, the Firdell 'Blipper'™ radar reflector, which had been uselessly taking up space in the forepeak for some weeks, was fitted to the mizzen mast. There had been an old-fashioned 'raincatcher' reflector there but we had been convinced by what we had read and heard about the trials of various types of reflector that the plastic sausage stuffed with metal material showed up better on a radar screen. We have occasionally asked friends with radars to check our reflection and the results have always been positive. We've been told that we look like a super-tanker proceeding at five knots.

We were almost sorry when the wind finally moderated and we were able to leave Salcombe. Our departure wasn't entirely without excitement because we decided to fill up with fuel before we left. Just before nine o'clock in the morning we motored from our mooring down the estuary towards the fuel barge in the middle of the harbour. As we were positioning *Nyala* to come alongside the barge against the tide the engine cut out, leaving us drifting crab-wise. It became apparent that we were going to narrowly miss the barge and it was too early in the morning for the attendant to be on board to grab a line.

'Anchor!' I shouted, but David thought more quickly. Grabbing one end of a mooring line he ran along the length of the bowsprit and leaped onto the fuel barge. He's not normally an athletic type but it's amazing what adrenalin will do.

It took him half an hour of angry investigation to discover why the engine had stopped. It was quite simple. While he'd been working in the bilges he'd knocked the tap of a fuel filter into the OFF position. There'd just been enough fuel in the system to take us from the mooring to within jumping distance of the barge.

When we finally got under way we had to motor all the way back to Exmouth in a flat calm. I have to admit that after all the alarms and excitements it was quite a relief. We struck the tide exactly right in the mouth of the Exe, at half-flood, and made our way up the complicated approach channel on a curiously quiet spring evening just as the sun was dropping towards the distant familiar hills.

There was no flotilla of small boats waiting to greet us after our desperate passage, no band on the pier, no cheering friends on the esplanade. But we were passed by a single boat, the port's water taxi, hurrying home after a late job. It was driven by a friend, a man who knows about boats. He throttled back his engine as his eyes flickered appreciatively over the lines of our little ship and he said, 'Is this her? Oh, but she's pretty!'

Chapter 7
Furnishing

On the next spring tide we beached *Nyala* in her mud berth, where David could rely on at least a week during the coming neap tide when she wouldn't float at all and he could sort out the leak problems. I was to get on with the next stage of fitting-out the forepeak with lockers and bunks.

To say that we beached her is to gloss very quickly over the time we spent arranging lines and anchors that could easily be picked up when we brought her in, and the nail-chewing tension as we manoeuvered her at high water out of the main river, through a spider's web of other people's mooring lines and up the narrow channel into the creek.

We knew that channel well. It wasn't the first time we had brought a boat up there but in the past they had always been dinghies or dayboats, or other people's yachts. Parking our precious *Nyala* half way up a beach was a different matter altogether. I won't say that we needn't have worried; it was probably precisely because we did worry and take a lot of care that the job went smoothly. Then we sat on board while the tide ebbed, adjusting the lines as necessary to make sure she sat as upright as possible on her new legs in the place where we had cleared all the stones off the bottom. In the end *Nyala* settled so well that she was able to sit in the creek throughout the rest of the spring and the early summer, where she looked so pretty that several local artists painted her picture.

I soon found that building furniture on a boat immediately presents some interesting challenges that aren't found in a house. While planning the work, my simple aim had been to finish up with the vertical and horizontal planes of the furniture at right angles to each other and so firmly fixed to the hull that they wouldn't move even under impact from a body or some other heavy article being hurled against them with considerable force. I already knew about the major problem: that the marine equivalent of an outside wall, to which all the furniture must be fixed, has no straight surfaces and that I would be attaching things to the continuous asymmetrical curves of the hull through three planes.

What really set me back conceptually was trying to arrive at some decisions about the bases of the horizontal and vertical planes without using the usual levelling tool, a spirit level, which just wasn't going to give me any reliable information on board. If I wanted the interior fittings to appear to present surfaces as near to the true horizontal and vertical as practicable when the boat was afloat, where was I to begin?

When *Nyala* was shored-up in the boatyard there was no way I could be certain that she was shored level. She could have been set down with either her bows or her stern up. The fact that the keel was level didn't necessarily tell me anything about how she would lie when she floated. Later when she was in the water I thought I had a better guide until I began to consider whether she would remain balanced and trimmed as she was then. Would we be adding any heavy weight fore and aft, port or starboard, that could affect this?

I soon realised that the starting point for these vertical and horizontal surfaces was only relevant to the appearance of everything else below-decks. It was up to me to determine where the true planes lay. However, once a decision was made I would be committed to that set of planes for the remainder of the fittings, otherwise the overall result wouldn't be pleasing to the eye.

There were two useful guides I was able to work from. *Nyala* has a large mast tabernacle support forward of the main saloon that does give the impression of standing vertical. Also, the companionway bulkhead and hatch appeared to offer horizontals and verticals that were satisfactory to the eye. I decided that these would be the constants from which I could begin to measure right angles.

My selection of materials was governed by what was already fitted in *Nyala* and by the large amount of wood that remained from pulling out the original forepeak lockers. For the parts that showed and those that needed strength I used iroko which is a good-looking wood that is cheaper and more readily available than mahogany or teak but just as durable. Its only drawback is that it is odd-grained – that is to say the grains are of irregular length and arrangement which sometimes makes planing, routing and sanding difficult.

For surfaces that were to be painted or hidden from view I used 1cm or 2cm thick pine tongue-and-groove, or 1cm exterior-quality plywood. The plywood was also used for shelves. For exterior finishing off I used some standard teak trims available from most chandlers or timber merchants.

The new forepeak arrangement was to include, tucked underneath the side-decking opposite the new heads compartment, a hanging clothes locker with front access and, in front of it, a half-height locker with top access for folded clothes (Figs 7.1 & 7.2). Forward of the tabernacle would be a double bunk with two large sail and equipment storage lockers, accessible from above, beneath the bunk mattresses. Then would come the chain locker and, forward of the Samson post which passed all the way down to be

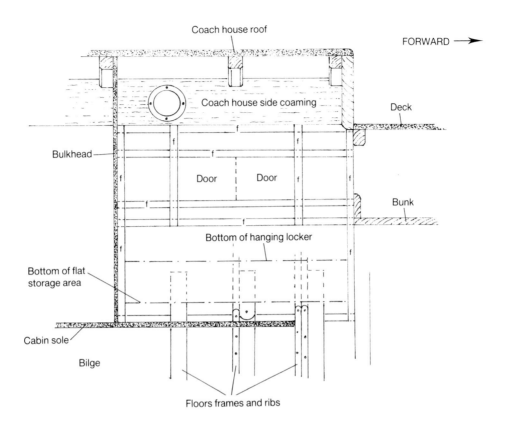

FORWARD ⟶

Coach house roof

Coach house side coaming

Deck

Bulkhead

Door   Door

Bunk

Bottom of hanging locker

Bottom of flat
storage area

Cabin sole

Bilge

Floors frames and ribs

f denotes 50 × 50mm hardwood frame.

Fig 7.1 Location and basic framework of clothes locker

seated on the keel, a spare flexible water tank. Because the space available forward of the tabernacle wasn't long enough to provide a comfortable fore-and-aft bunk we decided to position it thwartships, which means that one person has to lie slightly curled up or stretch out at an angle, but this has never presented any problem to either David or me and we are both tall people.

One very important aspect of the design was that the bunk was beneath the forepeak hatch, with access from both the deck and from the main saloon which we considered essential from the safety point of view.

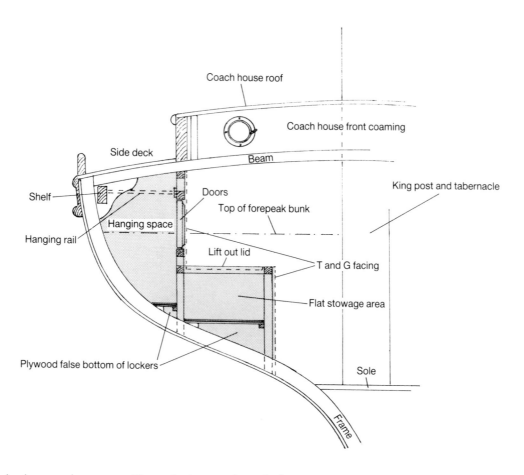

Coach house roof

Coach house front coaming

Side deck

Beam

King post and tabernacle

Shelf

Doors

Top of forepeak bunk

Hanging space

Hanging rail

Lift out lid

T and G facing

Flat stowage area

Plywood false bottom of lockers

Sole

Frame

Shaded area shows position of plywood end pieces.

Fig 7.2 Cross-sectional view of hanging and flat stowage lockers

Although every locker that has to be made is slightly different in construction because of the constraints of its position and its intended use, the same basic sequence always applies of framework first, followed by interior fittings, and finally exterior finishing. The first part of this locker construction was to make a framework of supporting battens, using 4 × 4cm hardwood. Figure 7.3 shows this framework and the basic joints used. Every joint had to be mea-

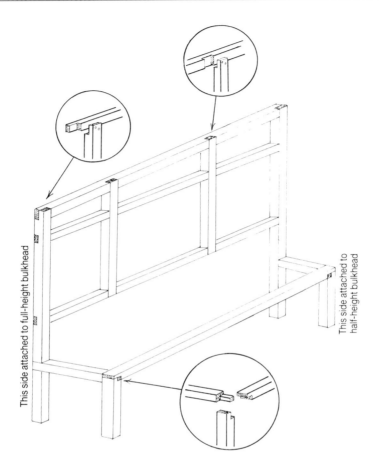

This side attached to full-height bulkhead

This side attached to half-height bulkhead

Angles are exaggerated to highlight the problems of joint cutting.

Fig 7.3 Frame for clothes locker showing joints

sured, cut with a tenon-saw and put together 'dry' to check the fit, remembering to take account of those difficult angles dictated by the shape of the hull. This was a tedious and time-consuming part of the job but it was important to get it right and to fix nothing permanently until everything was worked out and ready to go in place. When I was satisfied that all the joints fitted and the pieces were the correct lengths, the framework was screwed and glued in place.

I began by fixing the pieces that adjoined the bulkheads already standing – the full-height one at the end of the saloon and a half-height one between the tabernacle and the hull which marked the end of the clothes locker and the beginning of the bunk (Fig.7.1) – and I worked from these bulkheads towards the parts with less support.

The next thing to consider were the internal fittings, the hanger-rail and the side battening for the floor and lid of the flat storage box (this battening could have supported shelves in the case of another kind of storage locker). If you are a contortionist or a dwarf it is possible to get these internal fittings into place later, after the front of the locker has been built, but I found it to be much easier at this stage.

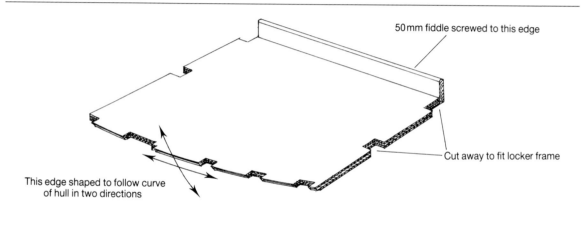

50 mm fiddle screwed to this edge

Cut away to fit locker frame

This edge shaped to follow curve
of hull in two directions

Cut away to fit frames and ribs

Fig 7.4 Locker shelves

In a later locker in the galley, the shelves I was building had to be supported on the framework and extended to the back of the locker, resting on the curves of the hull, where they had to fit round any ribs and frames that were in the way. Such shelves are always a very irregular shape (Fig. 7.4); measuring and fitting them isn't easy so paper or hardboard patterns are essential. With the confidence won through my earlier success with the bulkhead, I started with a straight edge similar to a spiling board and measured towards the hull, using the contour gauge and the sliding bevel to determine the curves.

When I was satisfied that I had mastered the correct shapes, I cut out the shelves and before fixing to the battens with glue and screws, attached to the front edge a 'fiddle' – a strip of wood that protruded about 2cm above the shelf to prevent the contents evacuating themselves if the door should be opened while the boat is heeled. I remembered to make the shelf small enough for the doors to close over the fiddle.

Back in the hanging clothes locker, I screwed the necessary 2 × 2cm battens in place to support the floor and lid of the flat clothes-storage box (Fig.7.2). Then I made two small plates to support the hanger-rail, fixing one to the shelf (that part of the boat's frame that supports the side-deck and shouldn't be confused with shelves for keeping things on), and one to the inside of the locker frame (Fig 7.2).

Once all these internal fittings were in place the next stage of the job, the exterior of the locker, was straightforward by comparison. It consisted of glueing and screwing the front faces of the lockers in place on the framework. Using tongue-and-groove I was able to insert each piece in turn, double-checking and adjusting for those curves top and bottom, and of course working around the door openings. The wood had to be set 2cm back from the edge of the frame around the door openings, to leave room to attach the door frame (Figure 7.5). There were the usual problems adjusting to the curves and working around the frames and ribs, in places where any of these front faces fitted to the lower part of the hull. All these protuberances are so essential to the construction of the boat but incredibly irritating when installing fittings (See Fig 7.1).

Where the finish of these front faces was to be painted I inset the screws about 5 mm, and faired these holes with filler (International's Interfill 100). In places where I was intending a varnished finish I plugged the holes with teak plugs bought by the hundred from most timber merchants. It is possible to make your own with a plug cutting drill attachment but I thought I had enough to do at the time.

Once the front faces were in place the flat storage box was built, adding battens to the front of the hanging locker to support the floor and lid of the box, then adding the outer front, again of tongue-and-groove (Fig 7.2). I also had to fit a small plywood end-piece to the forward end of the hanging locker, above the level of the bunk. The lid of the storage box was cut out of a single piece of ply, drilled with holes for finger pull rings and embellished with a moulded quadrant around the edge.

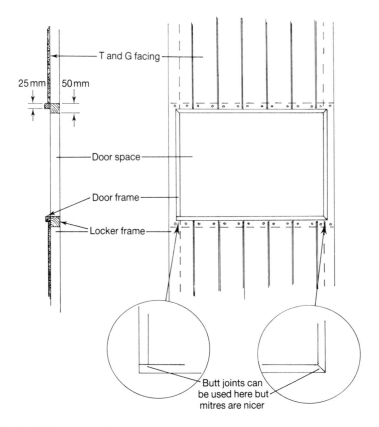

Fig 7.5 Showing the tongue-and-groove facing cut and fixed
to allow the door to be attached to the frame

Next the door frames had to be fitted into the spaces left for them.
These were cut from hardwood to match the doors and glued and
screwed directly into place against the locker frames (more plugs
over the screw holes). These frames can either be butt jointed at the
corners or mitred (Figure 7.5). I have tried both methods and I think
the mitres look better.

Lastly the doors had to be fitted. The selection and fitting of doors
presents a completely new set of problems which I'll come to in the
next chapter. Before that I continued into the forepeak to make the
bunk and the lockers underneath it.

I'll start this description by stating quickly that I first had to put

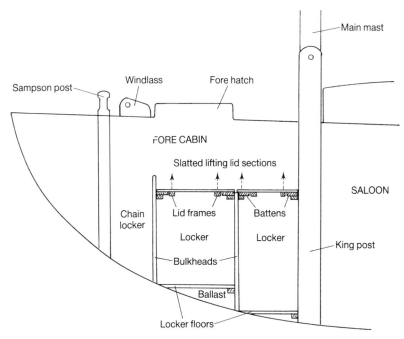

Fig 7.6 Forepeak showing bunk frame and lockers

in two more half-height plywood bulkheads across the full width of the hull, one to divide the forward end of the bunk from the chain locker and one half-way across the bunk to divide the considerable locker space underneath it (Fig. 7.6). I was getting better at the bulkhead job by then, but it still didn't proceed entirely quickly or smoothly.

After that I had to fit a hardwood frame to support what were to be the slatted locker top and lids – slats would allow the air to circulate beneath the mattress and around the contents of the lockers. I started by screwing and glueing battens to the top edges of the bulkheads, then matching them with fore and aft battens that were screwed to pads glued against the ribs and frames. On top of these battens I fixed a 6 × 4cm hardwood frame, jointed at the corners, with an additional hardwood fore-and-aft support in the centre of the widest part of the locker, from the central bulkhead to the tabernacle. Once this outer frame was fixed in place I had to build and make joints for an inner frame that would support the locker lids. (Fig 7.6)

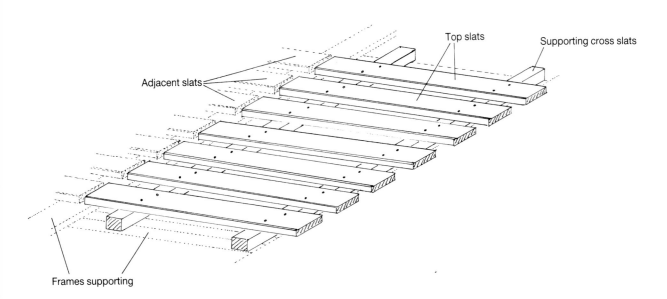

Adjacent slats

Top slats

Supporting cross slats

Frames supporting

Fig 7.7 Construction of slatted lid to forepeak locker

Making the locker lids and slatting around the edges of the lid holes was simple, but time-consuming. Each slat was 4 × 1.5cm pine and I planed off a slight bevel on each of the two top edges. The lids were made by joining the required number of slats, cut to the right length, by two cross slats on the underside. These cross-slats had to be positioned so that they were far enough in from the outer edges to allow the lid to rest on the framework (Fig.7.7). Each place where the cross-slats met with the main slats had to be fixed with two brass screws.

Before I fixed the surround slats to the top framework of the locker, where the length of each slat had to be individually mea-sured and cut to accommodate the curve of the hull, I fitted the two lockers with plywood floors that would keep their contents away from the bilges and make sure they remained relatively dry and clean. In theory these floors were simple to make, they needed no battens because, if measured and cut correctly, they would rest on the curve of the hull (Fig 7.6). This involved more spiling and pattern-making, cutting around ribs and frames and sanding off the angles to allow for the vertical curve in the thickness of the plywood I was using.

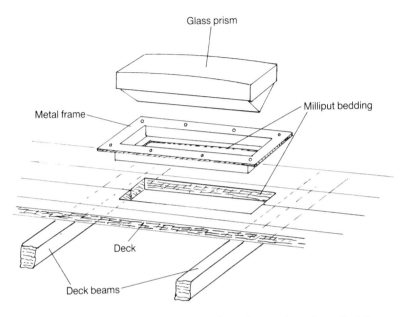

Glass prism

Metal frame

Milliput bedding

Deck

Deck beams

Fig 7.8 General arrangement of rectangular deadlight

When all the woodwork seemed to be finished I painted the whole forepeak in white gloss, then as a finishing touch I screwed 20 × 2cm iroko varnished side boards to the top battens of the two bulkheads that represented each side of the bunk, to hold the mattress cushions in place.

One disadvantage that quickly became apparent with this whole arrangement was that the forepeak was rather dark unless the hatch was open, which in a northern European climate wasn't always convenient. We quickly decided to fit two deadlights in the foredeck, though I wasn't totally convinced at first that making large holes in a watertight deck was a good idea.

From the many available in Davey and Company's catalogue we chose two 22 × 8cm rectangular prisms in galvanised frames. The advantage of prismatic glasses is that they let in far more light than their actual size would allow if they were flat glass. When these arrived it was obvious that whilst fitting the frames into the deck would be a simple job, fitting the glass prisms into the frame might be more of a problem. I had sort of imagined that once it was screwed down the frame would hold the prism in place but in fact what had to happen was that the frame would be firmly secured to the deck and the glass dropped into the frame (Fig 7.8) and secured around the edges – with what? Would putty be strong and enduring enough to prevent the prism being scooped out one day by a heavy sea?

I telephoned Davey and Company and, in their view, it would, although they added that many boatbuilders liked to fortify their putty with either red and/or white lead, or tar, or some other bituminous substance. In a more modern vein they recommended silicon mastics or two-part polysulphide mastics.

Our solution was to use our favourite Milliput™ two-part putty, which is a polyamide-based product. Its advantages are that it sets in damp conditions and is much harder and more adhesive than ordinary putty; also, it doesn't eventually shrink in the way that putty does.

Before cutting the holes in the deck it is important to measure out the position from below in order to make sure that you miss interior fittings such as deck beams, bulkheads and electric wiring. These measurements should then be transferred to the outside because cutting from below is usually cramped and awkward.

Once the cutting lines have been marked on the deck – make sure they are to the smallest part of the frame, not the outside of the overlapping lip – 10mm pilot holes have to be drilled at each corner of a rectangle, or in just one position if a circular prism is being installed, into which a saw blade – electric jigsaw or hand keyhole saw – will be inserted. It's important that these holes are on the inside edge of the cutting line, e.g., the part to be discarded, and not bisecting the cut (Fig. 7.9).

It's as well to check what or who is underneath when these holes are being cut in the deck because it's impossible to prevent the pieces of wood you have cut out from obeying the laws of gravity and plunging into the depths below.

The galvanised frames fitted easily but not too closely into their holes and the next thing was to drill pilot holes for the screws in line with the holes in the frames. Then they were lifted out and bedded back in place with the Milliput two-part putty, using the screws to pull down the frame tightly onto the deck before scraping away any excess Milliput. Then I lined the frames with a fresh mix of Milliput and pressed the glass firmly into this until the underneath edge of the glass almost but not quite touched the frame, then again scraped away all excess Milliput.

The final stage of the job was fiddly and almost unnecessary. I thought that from below the join between the frame and the deck

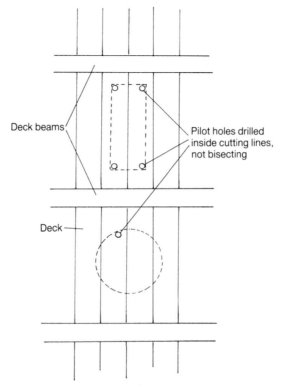

Deck beams

Pilot holes drilled
inside cutting lines,
not bisecting

Deck

Fig 7.9 Cutting lines and pilot holes for rectangular and circular deadlights

looked rather untidy and because it was above my bunk I would be spending quite a lot of time looking at it. So I fitted small mitred frames made of 5 × 15mm strips of pine, tacked and glued into place.

All this interior fitting went on in a logical progression but it turned out to be far more complicated and take far longer than we had at first imagined, and other people I have spoken to have had the same experience. The work is not helped by the assistance of an army of small gremlins who hold the tape-measure crooked, kick boxes of screws into the bilges and jump onto the flexible glue container, to mention but a few of their tricks.

But all these hazards, all the skinned knuckles and torn fingernails and bruised scalps, faded into insignificance as our friends and relations, visiting to inspect our progress, said in amazed admiration, 'You didn't make that, did you?'

Chapter 8
Making Locker Doors

It follows that once lockers have been made to keep things in, there has to be some means of closing them and making sure that they stay closed when they're meant to. At first I thought that I would simply be able to go along to some DIY shop and buy little doors that would then be hung or slotted in place in frames that had been built to accommodate the difference between the sizes of the doors and the sizes of the holes they had to fit, in much the same way as I'd always proceeded when making fitted-cupboards in a house.

I was rather put out when I couldn't find anything ready-made that exactly matched what was already in place in *Nyala's* saloon and certainly nothing that was anything like small enough to adapt to fit the strange variety of locker sizes we were going to end up with. So, with a misplaced confidence that seems to me in retrospect to have been bordering on the lunatic, I took out my pencil and paper and studied the doors already in place, eyed up the pieces of iroko in the workshop and declared my intention to make the necessary doors from scratch.

This was inspired either by extreme dedication or pig-headedness, according to whether you are the party who believes that nothing but the best is good enough for *Nyala*, or the one who is bearing the brunt of the suffering that is going on in the workshop and believes that there is such a thing as going over the top. It is greatly to David's credit that he said very little, but kept a careful eye on what I was doing and made one or two gentle suggestions at key stages.

The basic design, shown in Figure 8.1, was comparatively simple, especially after those bulkheads and lockers. I used 2.5cm-thick iroko to match *Nyala's* interior but it needn't have been quite as thick, I was simply using what we already had in stock.

The job was started by cutting and rough-planing the five pieces needed for each door – two stiles (uprights), two rails (cross pieces) and the central panel (Fig 8.1). The relative proportions were governed by the size required for each door and the size of the plank I had available. For one door wider than the others I cut wider stiles to avoid having to join two pieces for the central panel but there would have come a point where this would have looked out of proportion and the central panel would have needed to consist of two pieces tongued-and-grooved together.

I cut all these first pieces generously, knowing that they could easily be trimmed down when the doors turned out to be too large

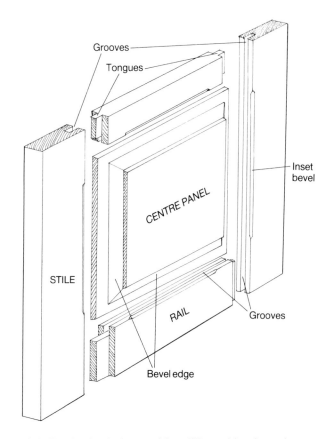

Grooves

Tongues

Inset
bevel

CENTRE PANEL

STILE

RAIL

Grooves

Bevel edge

Fig 8.1 Exploded view of traditional locker door

for the frames but that if they were too small making them larger would be a different matter.

The design for doors may be simple but some of the work involved is quite complex and whenever I came to a process I had never before attempted I made a practise piece first, several times if necessary, using the same type of wood as my finished work because by then I had discovered that tools often work differently in different types of wood.

The next job after the planing was to mark on every piece the places where I needed to cut the bevels on the central panels, and the tongues-and-grooves. This was fiddly and time-consuming but it was essential to be as accurate as possible right from the start.

Cutting grooves in door rails with plough plane.

To cut the grooves, I clamped each piece in turn into the top of the Workmate, then set the plough plane to the correct distance from the edge and the correct depth of groove. Starting gently because the first few strokes of the plane are the most important to get right (which I learned the hard way), I ploughed away. This is hard work but the results can be very satisfying. If necessary (which it often is) the inside of the groove can be tidied up with a sharp chisel.

Next I cut the tongues in the ends of the rails which was comparatively simple. I clamped each piece firmly to the Workmate with a G-cramp and, laying a straight piece of wood along the cutting line as a guide for the first few strokes, cut down with a sharp tenon-saw. I could then clamp the piece upright and make another cut with the saw at right angles. However, I later found it easier to shave out the right-angled piece with a plane. This only takes a few moments and is less dangerous and difficult than sawing down into the grain. Fig. 8.1 shows the grooves on long edges of the stiles and rails, and tongues at the ends of the rails.

After that I proceeded to the fancy stuff, cutting the bevel edges to the central panel (Fig 8.2). For the sake of appearance, to match up with what was already on the boat, I cut a wide bevel on the front of the panel and a narrower one on the back. For this job the practise pieces were of utmost importance as I could easily have ruined a whole panel with one false stroke of the plane.

Cutting bevel edges to central panel with electric plane.

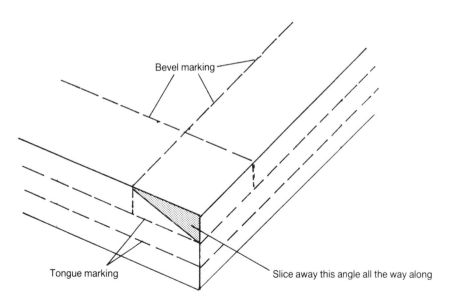

Bevel marking

Tongue marking

Slice away this angle all the way along

Fig 8.2 Marking out central door panel for bevel and tongue

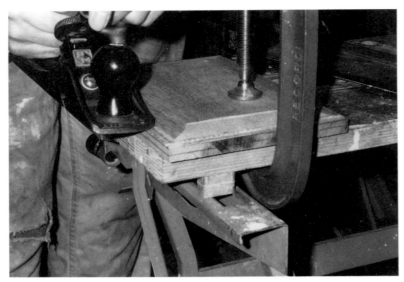

Trimming down tongues on central panel with bench plane

I began with the front bevel and with a sharp tenon-saw I cut a shallow guiding line along the line that I had already marked 2.5cm in from the edge. Then using the electric plane I cut the bevel at an angle between this guide-line and the line I had marked for the tongue on the outside edge (Fig. 8.2). The electric plane is a fierce tool demanding a steady hand and eye (to say nothing of a cool nerve), but the results look good.

I squared away the outside edge of the bevel into a tongue (Fig. 8.2) by making a cut down with the tenon-saw approximately 5mm in from the edge and then planing into the right angle with the hand plane as for the previous tongues I had cut.

After turning over the door panel, I cut in the back the right angle for the tongue, using tenon-saw and plane in the same way as on the rails. I also cut the small bevel on the back of the panel with the right angle bevel cutting guide on the electric plane, which was another job requiring steady nerves. The last bits of cutting to be done were the decorative inset bevels on the inside edge of the rails and stiles (Fig 8.1). These were done with a narrow chisel.

The door was now ready for glueing. I used WEST SYSTEM (but it could have been SP) epoxy mixed with brown micro-balloons, now called '407 Low-density Filler', which made any slight gaps in the joints totally invisible.

'Gaps in the joints?' I hear you ask, shocked. Well, you try it. It's back to this business of being an amateur and not expecting too much. By the time I'd finished I could turn out a perfect door every time but I won't need to for years to come.

Using such a strong glue may be overkill for making little tiddley doors, just as 2.5mm thick wood is, but I couldn't help thinking that I wanted my doors to endure if they were attacked by flying objects or leaned upon heavily. The instructions for using two-part epoxies say that you should first apply a thin coating on all cross-cut edges to be glued, and on all edges if using an oily wood such as iroko. After that, for the actual gluing I mixed the epoxy with the micro-baloons to the consistency of lumpy porridge.

Logic dictated that the first pieces to be glued would be the rails to the top and bottom of the panel. Having coated the tongues and grooves with glue I pressed them together gently and laid them on the workbench on top of a piece of clingfilm. The clingfilm prevents the work sticking to the bench by accident. If this does happen with epoxy glue, work and bench can be very difficult indeed to separate. I know because I did it once and in the end I had to sand part of the bench off the dinghy centreboard I was making. I also covered the top of the work with clingfilm before cramping across with sash cramps.

In order to make sure that the door would set flat rather than in a bow shape, I laid two pieces of spare wood on either side of the sash cramp and clamped them to the workbench with G-cramps. I put far more downwards pressure on these than I did on the sash cramp, which only needed to hold the pieces gently in place while the glue set. When the rails had stuck firmly, it was time to repeat the process with the stiles.

In general this glueing process was relatively trouble free, though I needed to chip some of the dry extruded glue away to smooth the edges where the first joint had been glued. However well I tried to wipe away the wet glue from the joints some always oozed out during the setting process, leaving a certain amount of chipping and sanding to be done. I found the Sandvik steel sanding plates particularly useful for this process.

Once the second glueing process was complete the work was ready for sanding. For initial sanding of hardwood I have found Sandvik steel sanding plates of various sizes ideal. For finishing I use various grades of Diamond Abrasive Aluminium Oxide sheets, sometimes with a power sander but often by hand for corners and curves where a power sander is inappropriate. In fact, I'm a bit of a nut about sanding good wood by hand. I have a theory that power sanders tend to damage the surface of the wood – certainly they do when someone tries to level a flat surface with a circular sander or tries to use them to remove old paint or varnish instead of working with heat or chemical stripper. A better finish is almost invariably achieved working by hand, either with or without a sanding block. It takes very little longer and is certainly no more of an effort than pushing a heavy, vibrating power tool back and forth. Anyone who doesn't believe me should give it a go someday.

After this sanding I took the doors, which were by now beginning to look very impressive, to the holes I proposed to hang them in and tested them for size. The official term for this is 'offering up' which always makes me smile as it does seem like some sacrifice to fate. Will they really fit?

There were inevitably small adjustments to be made, particularly to the angle of the edges that meet in the middle when the doors are closed. These cannot be right angles. They should either be contrarily angled, allowing the outside door to trap the inner one, or both angled slightly away from each other so that the only place the two meet is the outside edge (Fig. 8.3).

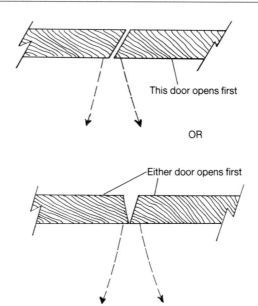

This door opens first

OR

Either door opens first

Fig 8.3 Cross-section through doors showing (exaggerated) the two possible ways to cut the mating edges

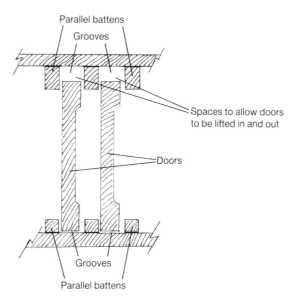

Parallel battens

Grooves

Spaces to allow doors
to be lifted in and out

Doors

Grooves

Parallel battens

Fig 8.4 Fixing arrangements for sliding locker doors

Once I had determined their exact fit the doors were ready to be sanded to their final finish, then hung.

At this stage it is possible to avoid the grief of hinges and catches by installing sliding doors in places where the opening are wide enough to allow for double doors. It certainly isn't a very complicated process making a double groove, top and bottom, to match the thickness of the door, allowing a slight overlap in the overall width, and making the door slightly shorter than the height of the hole so that it can be slotted into place (Fig.8.4).

This arrangement has the advantage that it takes up less room than doors that swing open but I find sliding doors for galley lockers to be irritating because, when I'm cooking, the ingredients I need in a hurry inevitably seem to be tucked behind the side of the locker with both doors drawn across it. Also, unless they are extremely well fitted, sliding doors do have the tendency to jump out of the grooves in desperate situations, just when you can do without the contents of lockers strewn around the saloon.

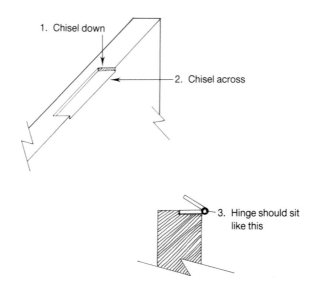

1. Chisel down

2. Chisel across

3. Hinge should sit like this

Fig 8.5 Rebating for hinges

It should be comparatively straightforward to hang doors with hinges but it seldom is. For a start, fitting hinges takes a long time. Each requires two rebates, one on the door and one on the frame, and has six screw holes to be drilled out and screwed into. This simply can't be hurried. The rebates need to be cut just the thickness of one side of the hinge, so that it lies flush (Fig. 8.5). Each rebate has to be marked, cut into the grain with a sharp chisel (after firmly clamping the door on its side), then the wood between the chisel cuts has to be shaved away gently.

Things can go very wrong at this stage, just when the end is in sight. For instance, if the door is slightly too narrow for the frame, the rebates may need to be shallower than the hinges. The door will still hang well but with a slight gap at the hinge side. If the frame is slightly twisted it may be necessary to rebate one hinge more than the other, and so on.

If by chance the rebates are cut a little too deep (and a lot of them are at some time or another) the door won't close at all, and it will be necessary to put a thin sliver of wood, or even cardboard, into the rebate to make the hinge stand out by the required amount. Real carpenters call these secret adjusting slivers 'soldiers' and I understand that they use them more than many would care to admit.

Another possible pitfall here is drilling the pilot holes for the hinge screws in the wrong place – it only needs a minute deviation from the correct spot to have a crooked hinge which will effect the hang of the door. If this does happen the only recourse is to fill the offending screw-hole by glueing a narrow wooden plug into it – matchsticks are good for this – waiting until it dries and starting again. With patience they always come right in the end.

The final stage was to fit catches. I had a wide variety to choose from: finger holes with internal catches, which are neat but the catches are difficult to install in exactly the right place; magnetic catches that are not a bit of good for boat lockers, they burst open at the slightest provocation and, because they are made of non-ferrous metal, they go rusty very quickly. Both for security and to match up with what was there, I adopted an old fashioned solution, a small bolt on the inside of the first of the two doors to close, and a brass twisting door latch on the outer door. These are easy to fix and are totally secure when properly closed.

Shortly after finishing these galley locker doors I had to make some more doors for the lockers in the new heads compartment. Because these weren't going to be on show they didn't have to match up with the style of doors in the rest of the saloon so I opted for a slightly simpler design. I made the central panel of plywood with no bevels, and rather than making grooves along the stiles and rails I fashioned them rather like picture frames with a right angle rebate at the back so that the central panel could just drop into place from behind, which presented a much easier fitting and glueing job all round (Fig. 8.6).

Although it sounds as though this business of making the doors just flowed smoothly on after I'd finished the other furnishing jobs, it wasn't really like that at all. They were done in little spurts of activity in between other things, started when *Nyala* was sitting on the mud in the creek near our house and completed a couple of months later when she was gracing her mooring on the other side of the Exe.

Some of the 'other things' involved earning our living and needn't be recounted here, some of them were far more interesting and important, like the dorade boxes with their brass cowls, and the varnish.

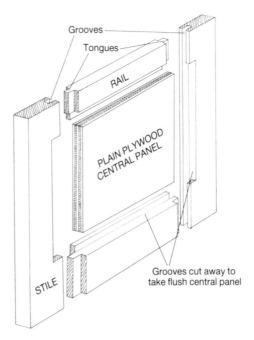

Grooves

Tongues

RAIL

PLAIN PLYWOOD
CENTRAL PANEL

STILE

Grooves cut away to
take flush central panel

Fig 8.6 Exploded back view of simpler version of door with plain central panel

The finished doors installed in the galley.

Chapter 9
Varnish and Ventilation

I think nobody could deny that if you own a boat varnish is important, even if only because it protects wood, but I expect a lot of people would wonder how it can be interesting. Fear of long, boring hours spent on varnish, or brightwork as it is called in traditional circles, is one of the things that puts people off owning wooden boats. This is a false economy because there is often a lot of woodwork to be varnished on modern yachts and the owners who say, 'Oh, I just leave it bare – I think the bleached wood looks so much nicer', are simply kidding themselves. It doesn't look nice at all, it looks like bare wood that nobody can be bothered to varnish.

Having said that I must admit that *Nyala*'s brightwork is not an easy option. She is to varnish what the Forth Bridge is to paint – there's always a bit that is pristine and a bit waiting to be done, and in between the two extremes most of it looks all right most of the time. This is because we have a system with varnish that has evolved over a time longer than our ownership of *Nyala*, starting with a sailing dinghy with foredeck and side decks so glassy with varnish that I was regularly ducked in the river because of lack of friction between my backside and the boat.

Because we lived in Exmouth, where they have been varnishing boats ever since the stuff was invented, our early efforts were subject to a lot of free advice. When the retired fisherman and boat-builder who was our neighbour walked past me the first time I was varnishing a small boat in our backyard he muttered through his teeth, 'Thirteen, Missus, you got to do thirteen coats to do a proper job, y'know'.

I suspected at the time that he was trying to frighten me rather than give me advice because it was one of his prejudices that no one ever does a 'proper job' on anything nowadays, but he did have a point. There is no substitute for patience in a varnishing job. The more coats that are applied, the better and longer-lasting the finish will be, but of course there's more to it than that. Just as important as brushing the stuff on is the way the surface is prepared, and what is done to it in between the coats, and afterwards.

In other words you get out of it what you're prepared to put into it and provided you don't skimp on the initial preparation, further maintenance becomes increasingly easy except in areas of heavy wear.

By now you may have gathered that we are prejudiced in favour of varnishing the traditional way, with lots of rubbing down and a great many coats. We are, however, quite prepared to acknowledge that there are other ways of going about doing the job. These alternatives include fast-drying two-part epoxy varnishes which only require two or three coats and which form a hard shell over the wood rather than soaking in. Or there is Deks Olya™, a Swedish wood oil designed with the freezing fastnesses of the far north in mind, which does even more soaking in than traditional varnish and which requires just as many applications to achieve a similar level of gloss. Choice of product and finish is very much a personal matter. We stick to 'traditional' varnish because we like the look of it, there's nothing to beat that lovely smell in the sunshine, and we find it easy to maintain in conditions that are sometimes far from ideal.

We know that what they nowadays sell, labelled as 'Traditional', isn't quite like the real old-fashioned stuff because it contains an ultraviolet resistant component and doubtless many other chemicals unheard of by our old boat-building friends in Exmouth. But owning a classic boat hasn't made us reject modern science, just use it with caution.

When we first bought *Nyala* her varnish was looking rather tired and I resolved that before the first year was out it would all be stripped off and replaced. There are three ways that I know of to remove dead varnish: heat, using an electric gun or a gas blowtorch; brute force, using an electric sander; chemical, using a proprietary paint or varnish stripper such as Nitromors™.

The first has two disadvantages. It tends to cook the underneath layers of varnish into the wood grain making it difficult to remove the last traces. Also, it is easy to cause damage either by scorching or, in the case of laminate and plywood, by the heat affecting the glue under the top surface and causing bubbling and/or delamination.

The sanding method seems quick and easy but even an orbital sander can damage large flat surfaces such as hatch covers by causing undulations. It's also easy to distort curves, rip plugs out and remove too much of the surface of the wood. Lastly, it's impossible to work an electric sander into corners around obstructions, though we understand that a new electric tool has recently been produced that does this.

The chemical method does a first class job of removing all traces of varnish without damaging the wood but it has the disadvantage of stinging the skin and damaging any surrounding paint or GRP or plastic with which it comes into contact. However, the water-soluble variety is easily wiped away with a wet cloth, and with rubber gloves and practice I found it possible to keep it under control.

I soon got into the habit of decanting a small amount of the chemical into some disposable container like a jar or an old food can and working from that. That way, if it's knocked over by accident there isn't so much damage or clearing up to do. I use any old paintbrush to apply the chemical – it's very good for softening up old brushes – and I find it better not to work too large an area at a time. It takes about five minutes for the varnish to soften and crinkle ready for scraping off. If it's left much longer it will harden again and be less easy to remove. I normally use a well-sharpened triangular paint scraper but any kind of scraper will do and it needs to be kept sharp enough – by filing – to bring the old material away cleanly but not so sharp that it scores the wood.

Two applications of the chemical are usually necessary to remove most of the varnish. When the wood looks 'clean', a final application of chemical, scrubbed in with one of those green pan scrapers will lift any remaining varnish from the grain. I used to use medium-grade wire wool for this but found that it tends to leave little rust stains all over adjacent surfaces which are impossible to remove. Then all traces of the chemical should be removed or neutralised by a wash down with fresh water.

The next stage is sanding – by hand, of course. I do two lots of preparatory sanding, first with 60 to 80 grade paper, then with 100 grade, but this does depend on the type of wood and how well it's been finished in the past. When the surface looks ready to varnish I go over it with a pan scraper dipped in white spirit. This lifts the dust out of the grain and, by briefly darkening the wood, shows up any lurking remains of old varnish.

Any dust on the surface or in the varnish when it's applied will spoil the finish so before turning from preparation to application it's important to remove from the surrounding area all trace of the dust caused by the stripping and sanding. This can be done either with a pan and brush, a vacuum cleaner or water; however, if any water gets onto the prepared wood it will stain and need to be sanded again, thus causing more dust – this could go on for some time! Before applying the varnish a final wipe over the wood with a clean folded rag or paper kitchen towel, soaked in white spirit, will ensure a dust-free surface. I know it is possible to buy specially prepared cloths for this final removal of dust but they have to be disposed of once they are loaded with dust and this becomes expensive compared to a kitchen roll and a bottle of white spirit.

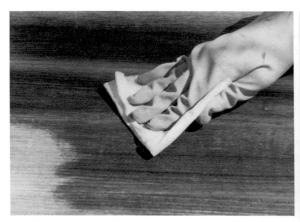

Wiping down the hatch cover with white spirit to clean off dust before varnishing.

Applying the first coat of very thin varnish.

I always aim to apply between eight and ten coats and not many of these are neat varnish. I begin with a mixture of real turpentine to varnish in a ratio of 20% varnish to 80% turpentine. Each subsequent coat contains about 10% more varnish than the last and only the top two coats are varnish straight out of the can. That way, the varnish in the early coats soaks into the wood and feeds it and bonds with the surface rather than sitting on top where it will crack and lift more easily.

Between each coat of varnish the surface is lightly sanded with a fine paper – 150 or 180 grade – to ensure a good key, and after each sanding is wiped again with white spirit to remove dust. To achieve a really mirror-like finish the last few coats can be sanded with very fine wet-and-dry paper.

I have found that it doesn't pay to try to apply more than one coat in a day even in good drying conditions because several coats applied immediately on top of one another as each goes touch dry don't seem to last for more than a few months. Freshly dry varnish remains 'green' for some time so although it's resistant to damp after two or three hours – except for the early coats where the high proportion of turpentine lengthens drying time – it won't take pressure, and sanding the new surface too quickly can damage it. New varnish won't take hard wear without damage for at least two weeks.

In this context, it was quite by chance that I observed that the jobs which were giving the best results in terms of resistance to damage and length of wear were those that had been interrupted due to bad weather, forcing me to leave some of the intermediate coats for several days before carrying on with the work. Allowing these coats hardening time seems to strengthen the finish and now, if at all possible, I deliberately let the job 'rest' for a few days after every third or fourth coat.

It's generally agreed that the best conditions for varnishing are a warm, dry, dust-free atmosphere and in winter this really means indoors. If there is no alternative to working in the open, windy days should be avoided as there's always either dust or spray in the atmosphere, so should boat yards which are inevitably dusty places. The best varnishing is done in gentle sunshine on a mooring or at anchor, well away from the shore, as long as there is no chance of spray in the air. A damp atmosphere will cause the varnish to 'bloom' – dry with a white opaque surface – which is a tragedy because then that coat has to be sanded off and done again. The old boatman's advice 'never varnish after tea time' is a good rule of thumb in order to avoid dew on the drying work, though it must be remembered that this means about three hours before sunset and can vary according to the time of year.

Most of our varnish lasts at least a year with no more attention than an occasional washing down with fresh water. I then make sure it lasts a good deal longer by some 'stitch in time' maintenance, which involves sanding down the surface and applying a further coat, even if it doesn't look as though it's needed just then. Even when those little grey speckles have appeared in areas of heavy wear, showing that moisture is penetrating into places where the surface has been damaged, the job can be 'rescued' by sanding the greying areas back to the wood and building up again with several coats, keyed into the surrounding 'good' varnish, finishing with a top coat over the whole area.

It's also possible to avoid decay by immediately applying a touch-up to any place that has taken a knock. We've heard of people who do this but I must confess that I'm more likely to look at it for days and even weeks telling myself that I'll do it tomorrow, until one of those tell-tale grey patches appears, then I'm sorry. Varnish really is an art in which a few minutes of timely attention will save hours of work.

I know that it will also save *Nyala* because every time the varnish has to be scraped right off and the wood sanded in preparation for a new application, a fraction of the thickness of the wood disappears. At 0.5 of a millimetre per year that's about sixty years before nothing remains of *Nyala*'s cockpit and coach-house but a heap of dust.

*   *   *

The whole of the first round of varnishing that frantic summer fell to me while David gave the rigging an overhaul and turned his attention to the question of ventilation below decks.

Having eleven opening scuttles, two hatches and a skylight, *Nyala* was, in fact, much better ventilated than most modern yachts but we were concerned that there would be times when weather conditions made it impossible to keep the hatches and portholes open without a lot of water getting down below. What we wanted was some kind of waterproof ventilation for the heads, the galley and the engine compartment.

We did already have one ventilator, over the galley, which was simply a hole through the deck with a plastic screw-down fitting over it. On one of my early occasions messing about with the rigging on deck, before we ever left Plymouth, I dropped the boom on this plastic fitting and broke it. At the time all we could do to keep out the rain was stretch a plastic carrier bag over the hole and keep it in place with a large jubilee clip around the stump of the broken ventilator. By some miracle of physics this bag stayed in place through several gales on land, the one in Queen Anne's Battery marina, and the one off Start Point. There was no way we could set off yet again and hope for the same kind of luck; it was obvious that a new and more reliable system had to be installed. The best idea seemed to be screw-down through-deck ventilators capped with dorade boxes with brass cowls and finished by varnished wooden trims inside the deckhead (Fig. 9.1).

This may seem to be an unnecessarily heavy arrangement but it's dictated by logic. The screw down ventilator allows the hole through the deck to be either open so that fresh air can be drawn in or stale air sucked out, or closed so that when there's a lot of water flying about nothing can get in or out, But in keeping out the water one also keeps out the fresh air whereas a dorade box cleverly keeps

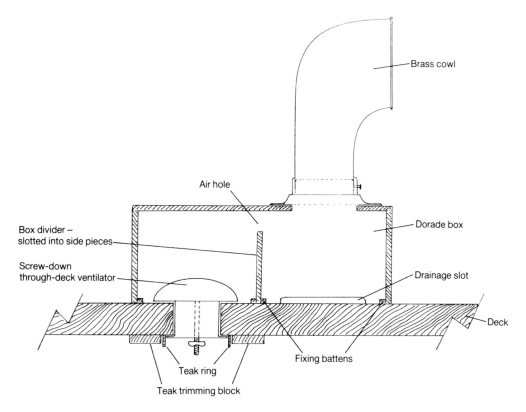

Fig 9.1 *Nyala's* system of through-deck ventilation

water out while continuing to let air in.

This is done by having two square compartments inside the oblong box, separated by a divider that has a gap at the top edge. One of these compartments has a hole on top through which air and water can come through the brass cowl, and slits at deck level through which the unwanted water can run away, but no access through the deck. The other compartment sits over the deck ventilator and allows passage to the air that comes through the gap from the first compartment (Fig. 9.1). Unless you are so unlucky as to have the entire first compartment fill with water right up to the top of the divider, no water will find its way into the second compartment and thence down below.

The cowl also has an important part to play, other than looking impressive. It can be turned so that its opening either faces the prevailing wind, or direction of travel, allowing fresh air to blow in; or it can face downwind or away from the direction of travel which allows air to be sucked out from down below.

The last part of the arrangement, the varnished trim down below which hides the rough edges of the hole through the deck, isn't strictly functional, but it looks nicer than a raw hole.

Anyone with a modern yacht can buy ventilators with integral dorade boxes but David had no choice but to make our own – and anyway, that kind of work gives him so much satisfaction that I doubt he could have been persuaded to buy anything ready-made however busy he was.

It didn't take him very long to cut out the six pieces for each of the three boxes and interior trims that we needed, from 1.5mm iroko. He joined the four side pieces with dovetail joints which I'm not sure wasn't simply showing off, but he says they were the most appropriate joints for the job, being strong enough to hold the box together in their own right.

Anyone who knows anything about dovetail joints will tell that they need to be practised. The idea is that along one of the two pieces to be joined a series of angled tongues are cut (the male part of the joint) and along the other a series of angled slots (the female part of the joint). The difficult bit is to get these tongues and slots fitting together exactly. First the outlines of the tongues and slots have to be measured precisely and drawn in pencil on the edges to be joined, using a sliding bevel or dovetail gauge. Then the wood is cut away on all three sides around the tongues with a dovetail or tenon-saw. The saw is also used to make the downward cuts into the wood for the slots, and a sharp chisel used to make the cross cuts, working from the narrow to the wide end of the slot (Fig. 9.2).

Next, David cut a 0.5 cm slot half way along the inside of each of the long sides, to take the dividing piece. Then the four sides and the dividing piece were joined together and glued with epoxy.

Where new through-deck holes were needed, these were cut to a 7.5cm diameter using an expanding bit with a hand brace. The screw-down ventilators were then inserted and screwed into place, bedded into Milliput to ensure a watertight fit.

Before fixing the boxes over the ventilator holes each box had to be individually shaped along the lower edges to accommodate the curve of that part of the deck it was to fit onto. It was important to remember that the compartment with the slots to let the water drain out musn't be the end of the box to be fitted over the hole.

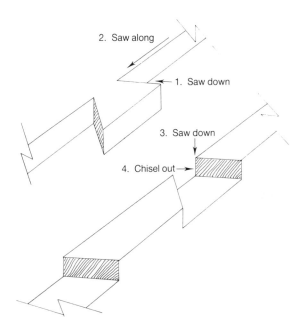

Fig 9.2 Exploded dovetail joint

The boxes were then fixed onto the deck with the small internal battens at each end, and each side of the dividing piece, glued and screwed first into the box, then down onto the deck (Fig. 9.1). The top piece was fitted last, remembering to put the end with the hole for the cowl at the opposite end to the hole in the deck, screwed and glued into place, the screws inset and the holes capped with wooden plugs.

A bit of preliminary varnishing was done before the collars of the cowls were screwed down over their holes, but the main varnishing was finished later.

Inside the saloon, square wooden surrounds with holes in the middle were glued and screwed in place beneath the ventilation holes, first scraping away the paint from the places where they were to be glued. These surrounds had chamfered outer edges and ready-made teak rings glued into the inner edges (Fig.9.1). Once varnished to match the other interior fittings they provided a neat and unobtrusive finish to the through-deck holes.

*   *   *

I have to record that as the weeks passed and *Nyala*'s beauty blossomed, David and I were becoming mere shadows of our former selves. We barely took time to eat and sleep, and housework or laundry or socialising with friends – unless they came to give a hand with the woodwork or the varnish – was out of the question.

People were saying that we'd never make it, never be ready in time. But we were determined. You see, it was no longer just a question of having everything working properly for our trip to France, everything had to look right as well because *Nyala* now had another date with destiny – she was going on The Telly.

Time for reflection – ship's cat and newly-varnished locker lid

112

Chapter 10
Upholstery and Television Crews

One of the many things that happened while *Nyala* was moored in the marina at Queen Anne's Battery, before the rudderless crossing to Turnchapel, was that she was spotted by a television producer.

The producer, who may have been called Chris, and an announcer called John, were busy filming in Plymouth for a series about the local sailing scene that was screened on the South-West television station. They had spent the day putting a big new go-faster yacht through her paces in Plymouth Sound, in unfriendly weather, and were returning the yacht to her berth in the marina when they saw *Nyala* and decided that at that moment she was far more to their liking than several tons of skittish plastic.

As soon as they could decently disengage themselves from the owners of the new yacht they hurried around the maze of the marina pontoons and accosted us, still clad in the grey and yellow designer drownwear that was all the fashion in yachting circles that season but, fortunately, quickly lost favour as soon as it was real-ised that a person overboard wearing grey and pale yellow becomes totally invisible in even a calm sea.

We invited them below for a drink which was obviously the right thing to do. As they warmed their cockles on red wine and their hands on the heat produced by *Nyala*'s new stove they enthused about traditional boats and yachting the way it must have been in the old days. Then and there they planned to do a programme about some of the old gaffers in the area. Would we mind if they filmed *Nyala*? They thought their schedule would require the pro-gramme to be made in July, probably in Dartmouth which was a nice central port along the coast to bring boats together from as far afield as Plymouth, Salcombe and Exmouth. They would be in touch.

We didn't exactly forget about them. We filed away July as being a nice deadline to have all the essential work done on *Nyala* so that we would be ready to go to France at the end of the month without a last-minute panic, and fit in a weekend of filming before we left.

In early June my work had progressed far enough for me to be thinking seriously about re-upholstering *Nyala*'s existing saloon cushions and making completely new ones for the double bunk I'd built in the forepeak. The foam for these two new cushions needed to be 10cm thick and cut to special shapes to fit the bunk so I made paper patterns and took them to the Foam Shop in Exeter. It's always better to get these pieces professionally cut by the suppliers than do it yourself because they make a much neater job of it and don't normally make any extra charge. However, if it is necessary to cut your own foam an electric carving knife does it very effectively.

At the shop I discovered that, due to the introduction of new regulations, we now had no choice but to buy the more expensive non-flammable foam. They were no longer allowed to sell the older type that caught fire rapidly and produced clouds of toxic smoke. Once we'd got over the shock of the extra expense it didn't seem a bad idea to have non-flammable foam in the cabin of a small wooden boat, specially when it's lit by paraffin lamps and one of the crew is a heavy smoker.

I wrestled with my conscience about whether we should replace all the foam upholstery with the new type and when I finally stripped the old material off the other cushions, the decision was made for me. The old foam had hardened and was messily crumbling away as I worked. The following day I was back at the foam shop with more measurements and paper patterns and then on my way round the upholstery fabric shops to gather samples of material for making the covering.

There is a school of thought that says that all the interior upholstery in a yacht should be covered with waterproof material. This undoubtedly makes it easier to dry everything out if the interior does get drenched but in my experience even the porous variety that is supposed to 'breathe' isn't very comfortable for everyday use. Especially in a warm climate, anyone sitting or lying on the cushions for a long period is soon hot and itchy through perspiration. I find it far more healthy and comfortable, as well as better looking, to use a heavy-weight domestic furnishing fabric that can be removed and washed when necessary and allows the cushions to air right through in the sunshine on deck when they do become damp.

Bearing in mind that we had already decided to have a dark and muddly print for the covers that would hide a lot of the potential stains we decided that what would look best with *Nyala's* dark varnished wood and traditionally-made furniture was one of the green, red and gold Victorian-style prints made by Laura Ashley. I had calculated that I would need twenty metres to do the job and of course, Murphy's Law being what it is – 'If it can go wrong, it will' – the Exeter branch of the shop didn't have that much in stock of the pattern we wanted. They could get it but it might take up to six weeks. Six weeks? Well, there was always a big demand at their factory and wasn't madam being just a little bit lacking in foresight to want to be supplied immediately?

Chastened, and thinking that as long as six weeks was the outside estimate, this would just about allow me to get the cushions made in time for the voyage to Dourarnenez, I placed the order.

In the meantime one of those extraordinary and unpredictable chains of events was already in progress that upsets the best-laid plans – what was that about Murphy's Law?

Bearing in mind the problems of security against theft for boats left unattended on moorings and in marinas, we had invested in a newly-marketed multi-purpose security system called Ultmar™. This was a set of sensors that detected fire, rising bilge-water, low battery state and gas leaks, for which it let off a standard alarm bell; it also had an intruder alarm, on the heat-sensor principle, which within a few seconds of an unauthorised entry made the saloon of the boat untenable by pounding the eardrums with a hundred and sixty decibels of high-pitched shriek. This is a noise of absolutely brain-mangling proportions as I learned to my cost one day when I fumbled the key and failed to disconnect the alarm within the allotted twenty seconds. The whole alarm system could also be connected to an aerial which would either buzz the owner at home if something was wrong, or send a signal to a control centre from which the police could be notified.

One of Ultmar's executives, Alan Smith, came to demonstrate the natty device to us while we were still in Turnchapel and over a few jars of ale in the Borringdon Arms he persuaded us that it would be worth parting with three hundred and fifty pounds in order to protect our investment from possible disaster. Not that we needed much persuasion, we were a truly soft sell; we'd already decided that we wanted the system and contacted him in the first place.

In due course the parcel containing the goodies arrived at our home in Exmouth together with a very complicated wiring diagram. David studied it, nodded and put it to one side to attend to later, when he'd finished dealing with the leak in the deadwoods and the hundred and one other little jobs waiting to be done.

At the beginning of June there came a telephone call from Alan Smith. 'How's your Ultmar?' he asked casually.

'Well, er . . .'

'Is it up and running yet?'

'Well, er, actually no, not yet. Haven't had time to get around to it.'

'That's a pity,' he said, and went on to explain that he had managed to get Television South-West interested in doing a feature on it and had told them that ours was an interesting local boat on which they could film it.

David asked if TSW had remembered they were coming to film us in July?

Alan said yes, they had. 'But they want to do it all in June not July. Haven't you heard from them?'

'Er, no. June's next week, isn't it?'

'That's right. Would you like me to come over one day and give a hand getting the Ultmar installed?'

'If you know how to do it, I think you'd better,' was David's reply.

And the same day we took a call from TSW who had managed to put two and two together and realised that they could actually save money by filming *Nyala* on one day for two separate features. Would we mind if the filming plans came forward to next week? Could we bring *Nyala* to Dartmouth over the weekend of 11-12 June?

'Yes? Great. See you there Saturday evening.'

Not only did Alan Smith do the installation job with a speed and efficiency that can only come from knowing the equipment inside out, he seemed to enjoy his day working on the river, popping over to the pub at lunchtime in the Tinker inflatable for a pint and a sandwich. When the work was finished we asked where we should meet him in Dartmouth for the filming.

Hesitantly, he said, 'I was just hoping . . . I know I'm not a very experienced sailor but I've done a bit. You wouldn't let me join you in Exmouth and crew for you over the weekend?'

Of course we didn't mind. Having a boat of one's own it's easy to overlook how much other people value a couple of days mucking about on the water.

* * *

I haven't forgotten about the upholstery, nor had I then. I was in a state of panic. How could *Nyala* possibly face her television debut with uncovered foam cushions in her saloon?

I telephoned Laura Ashley in Exeter, who seemed to have forgotten all about my order. I telephoned their next nearest branch, in Bath, only to find that they, too were out of stock of the pattern I wanted and all possible substitutes. However, they were a little better supplied in the sympathy department and they gave the telephone number of their head office in Wales.

A young lady with a frightfully well-modulated voice assured me that I wasn't the only person waiting for material in this particular design – several of their branches had run out. New supplies were on their way and I should be able to purchase some within a fortnight.

'That'll be too late!' I wailed. 'I've only got five days.'

'We can't possibly do anything for you in five days, Madam,' she assured me.

I took a deep breath. 'I need it sooner than that. I have to cut it out and make it up. Listen. I know this sounds like a tall story but I want it to furnish the interior of a classic yacht that's going to be filmed for television. I thought I had plenty of time but they've brought the filming date forward by a month. I did so want to use your fabric but if I can't get it I'll have to cancel the order and make do with something else.'

There was a brief pause. Then she said, 'How much did you say you needed?'

'Twenty metres.'

'Just a minute.'

It was actually less than a minute when she came back to the phone and said, 'If you can give me a credit card number you can have it by tomorrow.'

And an unopened, twenty-five metre bolt of cloth was on our doorstep by nine-thirty the following morning.

*   *   *

It took me two days to make up the covers. In sewing terms it wasn't a complicated job because, apart from a very few curves, most of it involved straight edges. The trickiest part was making contrasting piping to highlight the seams.

I have noticed over the years that many people who are competent craftsmen and have no difficulty in building a boat, fitting-out its interior and even making its sails, seem to draw the line at attempting upholstery. One well-known model of home-build boat that used to supply moulded hulls and decks and all the interior fitting in pieces for the home-handyman to complete, considered it necessary to supply the saloon cushions already made up, as though sewing was beyond the capabilities of a carpenter.

But in fact sewing and carpentry are both about problem-solving in three dimensions and, as I've said elsewhere, being able to sew gave me the confidence I needed when I first embarked on carpentry. The principle must apply in reverse – anyone who can successfully make things out of wood and handle wood-working tools must be able to sew, whether they realise it or not. And any sailor who can splice, knot and patch can also make covers, dodgers and awnings.

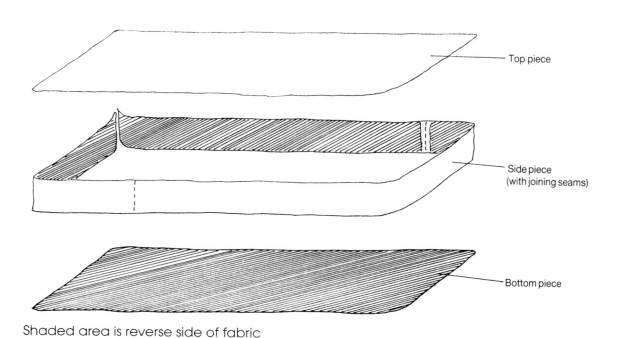

Top piece

Side piece
(with joining seams)

Bottom piece

Shaded area is reverse side of fabric

Fig 10.1 Exploded diagram showing fabric pieces cut for cushion cover

Each of the rectangular cushion covers I was making needed three basic pieces of material: one top and one bottom, which should be the same size as each other and accord with the size and shape of the cushion, and one side piece, the width of the thickness of the cushion (10cm in the case of those I was making for *Nyala*) and long enough to go right around the circumference of the cushions (Fig. 10.1). These pieces had to be cut large enough to allow an extra centimetre all round for the seam, but close enough to the measurements of the cushion as to make them a slightly tight fit round the foam interiors when finished. I knew that, like all cottons and linens, the fabric would stretch slightly in use and if the covers were too loose they would finish up wrinkling and forever working their way around the cushions.

Because the cushions were longer than the width of the cloth and I wanted the pattern to run cross-wise, all of these pieces couldn't be cut out of one width of cloth and I had to make neat joining

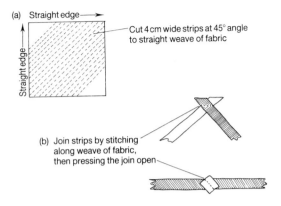

(a) Straight edge ⟶

Cut 4 cm wide strips at 45° angle to straight weave of fabric

Straight edge

(b) Join strips by stitching along weave of fabric, then pressing the join open

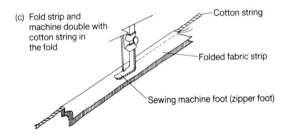

(c) Fold strip and machine double with cotton string in the fold

Cotton string

Folded fabric strip

Sewing machine foot (zipper foot)

Shaded area is reverse side of fabric

Fig 10.2 Making contrasting piping for cushion seams

seams in convenient places by placing together the two edges to be joined, right sides facing towards each other and patterns matching, and sewing a line one centimetre in from the edge, which was the seam width I had allowed for in cutting. Once sewn, this seam had to be ironed open flat to avoid unsightly bunching. If I'd been working with plain material I could have cut out with the fabric running the length of the cushions rather than the width and so avoided this joining process.

It would have been possible to make up the covers by simply stitching the three basic pieces together with no further refinements, but I knew that the finished job would look very much neater and more professional if a band of 'piping' (which is a little roll of material in either the same or a contrasting colour) was sewn into each main seam.

To make this piping I first had to cut out a series of 4cm wide strips, enough to make up the total length required. These strips had to be cut diagonally at forty-five degree angles to the weave of the material (Fig. 10.2a). This diagonal cutting makes the piping more flexible and more easily fitted around corners. These strips had to be joined into one long piece by stitching them, right sides together, and preferably along the straight edge of the cloth (Fig.10.2b). Once they were all joined the seams had to be ironed flat.

Then I doubled this long skinny strip of material over lengthwise and, using the one-sided 'piping and zipper' foot on the sewing machine, I machined a length of cotton string into the closed edge to make a little pipe, taking care not to stitch over the string itself (Fig. 10.2c). This stitching of the string into the fold of material can be done by hand with a running stitch but it takes a long time.

Then I pinned the piping into the correct seams by placing the two edges of fabric to be joined right sides together and placing the piping between them so that the raw edge of the piping met with the raw edge of the seam (Fig 10.3). If I hadn't been totally sure of my mastery of the sewing machine I would have pinned, or perhaps even tacked this seam together with long, removable stitches, before machining. In fact, I would probably have done several practise pieces first. In this way, 'piping' the seams as I went along, I sewed the top piece of the cushion all the way around its circumference to the side piece, taking care to ease (or bunch up) the stitching around the corners, and not to catch the string part of the piping with the needle. After that I repeated the process sewing the bottom piece to the other edge of the side piece, but I left open one of the long sides and stitched the piping along the top of this open side.

I turned the cover inside-out, ironed it, and fitted it onto the foam lining with a good deal of pushing and shoving and making sure that the corners of the foam were pushed well into the corners of the cover. I closed up the remaining open side by pinching the edges together, tucking the overlap underneath and hemming along it (Fig. 10.4). To be truthful, on the first couple of covers I left one of the short edges open because I thought it would be less work to hem by hand along a short opening than a long one. But I then found that it was far more of a struggle to fit the long sausage form of the cushion over the foam interior and so I opted for less work at that stage and a slightly longer hand sewing job.

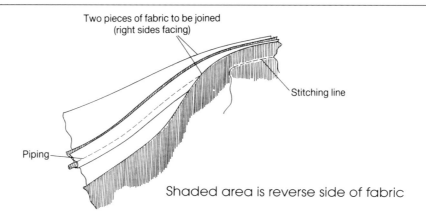

Two pieces of fabric to be joined
(right sides facing)

Stitching line

Piping

Shaded area is reverse side of fabric

Fig10.3 Joining two pieces of fabric with piping in the seam

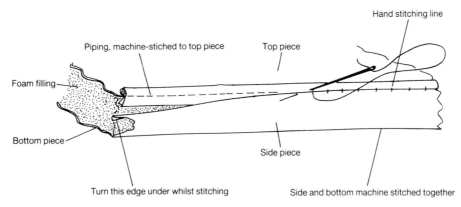

Hand stitching line

Piping, machine-stiched to top piece

Top piece

Foam filling

Bottom piece

Side piece

Turn this edge under whilst stitching

Side and bottom machine stitched together

Fig 10.4 Closing the final seam by hand stitching

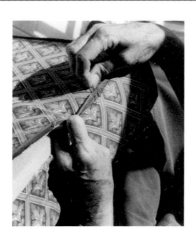

Hand-stitching the last seam on cushion cover – shows Laura Ashley fabric and contrasting piping.

Instead of stitching the covers closed I could have put zippers in but at the time I didn't know where to lay my hands on any long enough. I know now that it's possible to buy cushion zips by the yard and they do make it easier to remove the covers for washing. In that case I would have sewn one side of the zip into the bottom edge with the piping, the other side onto the turned-in raw edge of the side piece.

At the final stage I also had the option of studding the cushions by sewing on buttons at regular intervals, stitching right through the whole thickness of the cushions, to produce a quilted effect. This would have had the advantage of keeping the covers firmly in place but I considered that removing these buttons every time I wanted to wash the covers would make a lot of unnecessary work. Also, I don't find cushions finished in that way are comfortable to sleep on, neither do I like cleaning out the crumbs and fluff that invariably gather in the little pits around the buttons.

*   *   *

On the appropriate Saturday afternoon, proudly wearing her new livery and her new alarm system, *Nyala* set sail for Dartmouth and her appointment with fame. She covered the thirty nautical miles in fine style under all plain sail with a beam wind of twelve knots making it feel as though she was charging along like an express train. In fact, her speed in these conditions is between six and seven knots and on that sunny day, as the beautiful Devonshire coast slipped by, we felt as though she would take us anywhere.

The entrance to Dartmouth is one of nature's cleverer tricks and has ensured the prosperity of the town through the ages by making it a useful naval stronghold in times of war and a safe trading harbour in peacetime. It's a cleft between high cliffs and is totally obscured to anyone approaching from the sea until the very last minute. In fact if it wasn't for the Daymark, a tall obelisk on the top of the cliffs to the east of the entrance, it would often be impossible to find at all. Once inside, there is a deep water pool big enough to anchor several large ships in total shelter and beyond that a tidal river that winds several miles inland between steep wooded banks.

We guided *Nyala* into the bustling harbour with sailing dinghies dashing around, two car and passenger ferries plying back and forth across the river, tourist pleasure boats, a couple of anchored warships, a floating restaurant and several hundred yachts either moored or moving, all trying to occupy the same stretch of water measuring approximately one mile by a half adjacent to the town.

We made our way to the small marina at the top end of the town where a berth had been booked for us and before long were entertaining John and Chris and a young lady presenter called Sue. They outlined to us their plans for the filming the following day: in the morning we would sail *Nyala* in the Range, just outside the harbour, while they filmed and interviewed us. In the afternoon, moored in the marina, Alan would be interviewed on board about the Ultmar system. They were more confident than we were that we could handle the complicated sails and steer at the same time as facing a camera and an interviewer, but we decided not to worry. After all there was plenty of room out in the Range and if any problems arose we could turn *Nyala*'s bows seaward to sort them out.

Full of good cheer we rounded off a happy day with a good dinner in one of the many fine restaurants Dartmouth has to offer and forgot to listen to the weather forecast.

During the night I was woken by the sound of wind moaning in the rigging and I wondered how strong it would have to be before it was too rough to film in the Range. I wasn't too bothered about getting back to Exmouth – we could always leave *Nyala* in Dartmouth and collect her another day.

The following day dawned fine and sunny but still a bit gusty and we soon discovered that there was a very definite limit to how much rough sea the television crew would take, specially the sound engineer who hated boats only marginally more than he hated the human race and declared that anything larger than a small ripple was too rough for him. He had already done his own research and found out that it was very choppy in the Range which was enough for him to threaten to go on strike.

Someone made the bright observation that it was nice and calm in the river and wondered if we couldn't do the filming sailing *Nyala* up and down the river.

'All right,' David agreed. 'But only with the engine on in case of emergencies. And don't ask the Harbourmaster first.'

Once the decision was made some sort of invisible signal went out to a couple of neighbouring bars and about twenty people hurried purposefully out into the open, along the pontoon and boarded *Nyala*. As well as Alan, David and myself there were Chris and John and Sue, plus the sound engineer who didn't want to be there and an assistant sound engineer in case he suddenly wasn't there. Then there was an electrician whose job was to change the battery packs in the cameras and sound equipment, and his assistant, and a camerman and his assistant. There was a woman with a stop-watch and a clipboard and another who was probably her assistant, and several other spare people who vaguely said things like 'wardrobe', 'hair' and 'make-up' in spite of the fact that everyone was wearing their own very casual clothes and a blustery day on a boat in the middle of an English river is no time to be worrying about how you look. Apart from those of the crew who were moving purposefully about doing necessary things like checking the light and level of background noise, all the others arranged themselves along the top of *Nyala*'s coach-house in the best position to enjoy their sightseeing tour. As we drew away from the marina pontoon it was almost impossible to find a spare place on deck to coil the lines, and David couldn't see anything ahead from the steering position and so had to send Alan up to the foredeck to shout instructions.

'Right,' said Chris, once we were under way. 'We're going to sail up the river filming from the support boat and down again filming and interviewing you on board.'

'Support boat?' I asked, then David pointed out a small power dory that was following us. There was only one person in it – for some strange reason the driver had no assistant – so at some stage the camerman would have to transfer himself and his equipment and his assistant into this dory. The sound engineer was supposed to go too but he flatly refused to have anything to do with that part of the operation.

'Okay?' Chris asked.

'Not really,' said David. 'You see, the wind is blowing directly down the river and the tide is falling. There's no way we can safely sail *Nyala* up river because it'll mean tacking between the mudbanks.'

'What did they do in the old days?' asked Chris suspiciously.

'They went up on a rising tide so they wouldn't be stranded if they went aground. Today we can only sail going downstream with the wind behind us.'

'Okay, so we motor up the river and sail down with the camerman in the support boat, then we motor back up again and sail down again filming on board.'

'Fair enough,' said David and he turned *Nyala*'s bows up the pretty, twisted reach of the river above the town and I briefed Alan about the finer points of gybing a gaffer with running backstays. I also suggested that all the people sitting on the coach-house roof must go below into the cabin because one swing of the boom would send most of them straight into the water with cracked skulls. They complained that they wouldn't be able to see anything but Chris said he didn't want them on deck anyway, they would spoil his film. The only one apart from the cameraman and the still-grumbling sound engineer who was allowed to remain on deck was the assistant electrician. He had just told us that his father owned an old gaff-rigged boat and he turned out to be the most useful person on board because he knew exactly what was going on.

And thus *Nyala* came to sail majestically down the river Dart through the mêlée of Sunday morning traffic – twice. Chris worked hard to direct the cameraman to all the best shots – the water rushing past *Nyala*'s bows, Sue's unintentionally bare midriff as she reached up to pull on a halyard, David's masterful hand on the wheel. He hated to be interrupted. As we approached the first passenger ferry crossing point, wind and tide carrying us almost out of control into the busiest part of the river, Alan signalled from the bows that the ferry was approaching. It was a chain-ferry and unable to deviate from its course. There was no way we were going to be able to stop in time to avoid being swept down onto it. The only thing I could do was reach for the gear lever and increase the revs of the idling engine to a roar to get us past its bows.

The sound engineer signalled furiously to Chris who turned to me and demanded, 'What the hell did you do that for? You've ruined the interview!'

'It wouldn't have gone down too well if we'd put our bowsprit through the rails of the ferry,' I said. 'We'd have been on the news then instead of a feature programme.'

'Yeah, okay,' said Chris, not even flinching as he watched the ferry surging across our stern, hooting angrily. 'We'll dub it later, when we're tied up. Where're we going now?'

'Into the pool behind that battleship to take the sails down,' said David calmly.

'Great! Action! Camera, get them lowering the sails!'

It turned out to be a jolly good film, white bow-wave, interviewer's midriff, electrician crewman and all. Even David's interview turned out to be perfect – they cut out the bit where the engine roared and Chris shouted at me and the ferry hooted.

After that experience we felt ready for anything, certainly well up to getting *Nyala* across the English Channel and sailing in company with hundreds of other traditionally rigged boats while the organisers threw cans of Guinness and lager at us – but we haven't quite got there yet.

Chapter 11

Fog and Fire Below

We had arranged to have the whole of August free from other commitments so that we could take *Nyala* to the festival in Brittany and then spend a further week cruising south along the French coast before heading back home. Only then would we make the final decision as to whether she was the right boat for us to live aboard or whether we should sell her on and buy something else larger or easier to handle. I know we both hoped that she would be the one, that she wouldn't let us down or vice-versa but we had to face the fact that we hadn't yet been at sea in her for more than a few hours at a time nor, except for the week in Salcombe, had we sampled living in her confined spaces.

The Festival of Sail was to be a very special event, organised by the French magazine *Chasse Marée* in the bay off the town of Douarnenez, a town which boasted a maritime museum and an abundance of patience and goodwill. It was the second such biennial event; the first had attracted several hundred boats of various kinds of classic build and rig, and also a great many folk musicians and other interested but boatless aficionados.

At this second event there was to be hospitality for the visiting crews, free mooring, racing in the bay, boat-handling competitions in the fishing harbour, floodlighting in the evenings and a lot of side-shows and stands to spend money on. The entire town of Douarnenez was to be sealed off from the landward side so that everyone who didn't already live there would have to pay to get in to see the spectacle of the boats. The whole arrangement was a sweeping, grandiose concept and it was organised with a typically French vigour and efficiency.

We had no doubt that, being at that time fifty-five years old and still having her gaff rig, *Nyala* had a right to a place in the illustrious company that would include the Soviet sail training vessel *Boris Sedov*, the Bristol Channel Pilot Cutter *Hirta*, the J-Class racing yacht *Velsheda*, and our friend *Hoshi* from the Island Cruising Club.

The festival was due to begin on August 8th so we aimed to leave on the 3rd which we thought would give us plenty of time to make the passage to western Brittany, which shouldn't have taken more than between thirty and forty hours. That was our first mistake.

On the day we left the pressure was rising over the south of

England promising easterly winds, the same conditions that had prevented our passage to Exmouth earlier in the season. This time, however strongly it blew from the East we would be happy, *Nyala* would romp down the English Channel towards Ushant and the stronger the wind, the sooner we would be there.

Unfortunately nature had other ideas and we were treated to that other hazard of high-pressure conditions in those waters, flat calm and poor visibility. We motored out of Exmouth and along the coast as far as Start Point, where our course began to diverge from the land. Dusk found us fifteen miles out, approaching the inshore shipping lanes in gathering murk. One ship came to within a mile of us before we saw it and we began to hear others sounding their fog horns in the eerie stillness.

What faced us on that particular passage was at least twelve hours of crossing the busiest shipping lanes in the world, including one lane for giant supertankers travelling from Ushant to Rotterdam which are unable to slow down or deviate from their course for anyone. We knew from past experience that even in perfect conditions this exercise stretches the concentration of the crew of a short-handed yacht. In fog it's a suicidal undertaking even if everyone who is equipped with radar is able to watch it all the time. But friends in the merchant marine have told us that ships proceed up Channel at a steady twenty knots with only one deck officer during the hours of darkness, who has to attend to the ship's radio and charts as well as keep watch and monitor the radar.

All this adds up to the fact that shipping lanes in poor visibility are no place for a small boat; the only sensible thing is to be somewhere else. So it didn't take long for the chicken in our souls to triumph and wondering whether we were really psychologically fit to sail the world's oceans, we admitted our distaste for the situation that faced us and decided to turn back. David was navigating officer on that day and he was certain that even if the fog closed in as we approached the shore he could find the shelter of Torbay, tucked behind Berry Head with few off-lying dangers. Then he said, 'But the nearest place is Salcombe'.

'Oh no! Not Salcombe again!'

'It's only three hours away and as long as the vis stays like this we can get in easily.'

In fact it wasn't at all unpleasant being in Salcombe where we could socialise in the Island Cruising Club bar. There were a lot of people there who were, one way and another, on their way to Douarnenez and the most riveting topic of conversation was the coming weather. The good news was that the high would collapse in thirty-six hours and visibility would improve. The bad news was that the wind would then go into the south-west, right on the nose of any boat making passage for north-western France. It would become a fresh and helpful north-westerly later but not until August the seventh, the day the festival was due to open.

Having decided that our best option was to motor-sail as close as possible to the south-westerly, which was forecast to be not more than a Force four, we left as soon as there was a sign of the approach of the new weather system, late in the afternoon of the fifth. We had a filthy channel crossing.

We already knew from our earlier experiences that *Nyala*, while being a sturdy vessel, superb in heavy weather, could not be expected to take us easily on a windward passage. As anyone who has tried it will know, a shallow-keeled gaffer may point close to the wind but she won't go there. And the stronger the wind, the more she travels sideways through the water. So we had decided that, having an old-fashioned boat, our cruising would be of the old-fashioned kind, either going in the direction dictated by the wind or waiting until the wind was favourable for the direction we wanted to go. We would not have objectives that might be to windward, or timetables to be met. And yet here we were on our first long passage trying to make headway to windward to get to an event for which the opening date was three days away.

Nyala struggled on with the help of her engine, through a night and most of the next day of alternating drizzle and heavy rain. Sometime during the night we gave up trying to motor-sail. Tacking slowly amongst the shipping became too much for us and we lowered the sails and relied on engine alone. When the wind reached Force five, seventeen or eighteen knots true on the nose, our new Decca Navstar reported that even with the engine flat out we were only making one knot forwards through the water. Our only comforting thoughts were that at least we weren't going backwards and at least the engine was behaving itself now, not overheating.

We knew that we weren't the only people having a miserable passage. Every hour during the afternoon we crossed tacks with *Velsheda*. The great J-Class yacht, whose mainsail was larger than a tennis court, had no engine and she was trying to make the same passage as we were, sailing in long, wet tacks towards Ushant. We found it interesting that, with her sails up and her superb windward ability she was in fact making no better way than little *Nyala* chugging along in a straight line under engine.

Towards the end of that second afternoon, twenty-four hours after leaving Salcombe, the grey, cold uninviting line of the French coast came into view. We were planning to take the passage of the Chenal du Four, the rock-strewn channel between mainland France and the Île d'Ouessent, Ushant. In fact this channel is wide and extremely well-buoyed, quite safe for any boat following the pilotage instructions and often used by large ships. But the tide runs through it at up to nine knots so obviously a vessel only capable of five or six knots has to go through with the tide, not against it, which means timing an arrival at the first buoy of the channel, the Portsall, with some precision. As we struggled on towards the dusk it became obvious that we weren't going to make it, that we faced the longer journey round the outside of Ushant or several hours hove-to waiting for the tide to be in our favour again.

Then several rather alarming things happened at the same time. The first was a vicious squall with more wind and rain than we'd had all day, that finally stopped *Nyala* in her tracks. As the squall began to clear we saw, charging towards us over the horizon from the direction of Ushant, a veritable phalanx of supertankers racing for their berths in Rotterdam.

'We've got to get out of their way,' muttered David, abandoning our forward struggle and putting the helm over to turn us hard to port. 'Anyway, it doesn't matter now – we've missed the tide.'

Then suddenly the squall cleared and the wind changed.

'Look!' I yelled. 'The wind! Look at the wind!'

A classical cold front had just passed over and in minutes it had veered ninety degrees. We now had a fresh, steady north-westerly – a beam wind for the rest of our passage and enough to move *Nyala* into and through the channel before the tide turned.

'But we haven't time to put up the sails,' David muttered. 'I'd have to turn into the wind and we're still in the path of those tankers.'

'How long have we got?'

'Ten, fifteen minutes at most.'

'I can do it. I only need to get the main up. Give me a luff.'

The great mainsail slid up without any of the usual hitches and filled like the wing of a bird. David bore away and *Nyala* swooped across the swell and out of danger while I raised the small foresails and then, glancing forwards along the bowsprit, saw the Portsall Buoy balanced for an instant on the top of a swell not two miles ahead, marking the first turning point to go through the channel.

Triumphant but a little tired we were spewed out of the southern end of the channel a little after 22.00 hours, just as the tide turned against us. To reach Douarnenez we faced a further six hours of complicated pilotage but to our left lay the wide expanse of the Rade de Brest with the little anchorage of Camaret tucked into one corner, only two hours away.

We now had a day in hand and Camaret had the big navigational advantage of being a port we knew well enough to get into the anchorage in the dark. It seemed a good idea to rest up for a few hours and make the final passage the following day.

I had a further inspiration. 'I'll put our supper in the oven now and we'll eat it as we cross the Rade. That way all we have to do when we reach the anchorage is have an arrival toot of Scotch and go to sleep.'

So I went below to the galley, lit the pressurised paraffin cooker and put two tasty pre-prepared 'Country Kitchen' meals into the oven to brown.

Up on deck again I helped David to identify the next buoy, the unlikely sounding Swansea Vale that marks the wreck of a British ship. A few minutes later we heard one of the alarm bells of our Ultmar system ringing insistently. Hurrying below I saw that the fire alarm was flashing and the reason seemed to be that there was smoke issuing from the oven. Guiltily I remembered that I hadn't cleaned it last time I'd used it; there was probably something burning off the inside. I cancelled the warning light on the main panel and reported to David that it was a false alarm.

A few minutes later the bell rang again and, peering down the companionway hatch, I saw that the smoke looked more serious now, with little red flames licking at the base of the oven. There was a nasty smell of paraffin.

'We're on fire!'

I dashed down to confront the cooker, turned off the oven and grabbed the strategically placed fire blanket. But, jumping up and down and peering through the smoke, I couldn't quite see the best place to put it to smother the fire. Then I thought that if pressurised paraffin was seeping into the oven, the best way to stop it burning was to staunch the flow so I rushed out into the cockpit again, reached into the locker that held the paraffin tank, and turned off the pressure. That had no effect; if anything the fire was increasing and I realised that it might well take serious hold before all the paraffin that had already leaked out of the oven controls was consumed.

In the meantime, David was trying to maintain our course through a heavy curtain of smoke and my increasing sense of panic. He suggested that I try the dry powder fire extinguisher instead of dancing about with the fire blanket. Brilliant! But the extinguisher was at the forward end of the saloon, deliberately placed there so that someone could fight their way out if trapped below by a fire. I had to get to it past the now flaming cooker.

I put one foot on the top of the four companionway steps, slipped, and made the rest of the journey down the steps, past the cooker and along the length of the saloon on my backside. Adrenalin being what it is, I didn't feel a thing. I grabbed the extinguisher, held it at arm's length to focus it so that I could read the instructions – however often I read them in advance in calm conditions I never can remember them – pulled the pin and aimed the powder at the base of the fire.

Within twenty seconds it was out, much to the relief of both of us. But the cooker and our supper were a charred mess, neither to be of any use ever again. I'm a little ashamed to admit that both now lie at the bottom of the deepest part of the anchorage off Camaret, unless they've since been dredged up by some unsuspecting yacht's anchor.

Once we were anchored I scrabbled in the depths of one of the lockers for our spirit stove, saved from our backpacking days, and made us Cuppasoups for supper. But there my pioneering spirit came to an end. I wasn't game to cook on the single burner of the spirit stove for the next three weeks, so the following morning we went ashore in Camaret to exercise our very rusty French in search of a new boat cooker.

Camaret is a delightful seaside and fishing town with a small marina and two nice yacht chandlers but it's not exactly an international yachting centre and they don't have much call for boat cookers with ovens, which is what I was demanding. At first we decided that we would fit a new paraffin cooker – we liked the friendly glow of the brass fittings on *Nyala*'s old cooker so much that we were prepared to forgive its idiosyncrasies and the temperamental turns that came upon it from time to time. It only took us an hour or two to discover that we would be lucky to find a cooker at all in Camaret, let alone have a choice of model or fuel. To be sure, there were plenty in the shiny catalogues produced by M. le Couteur, the chandler, but they would all have to be sent for and we would have to wait a week or more for delivery.

Considering the language problems, they did very well to understand us when we explained our predicament: that we wanted a decent cooker but as we needed to get to the Festival at Dourarnenez and didn't want to spend our whole holiday without any means of preparing proper food, we wanted it right now. They also grasped the fact that we were unlikely to be fussy about how much it cost.

After a small hesitation M. le Couteur said, 'I seenk we have just what you want.'

'You have? Where?'

'Een Brest we are fitting out our own yacht – nossing but ze best, you understand. We have a gas cooker wiz offen still in its box, waiting to be fit. You can buy it and we order anosser.'

'Is it expensive?'

'Three thousand and nine-hundred francs, But you will lose ze tax and it is a very fine cooker. Made by ze company Electrolux, in Italy.'

Nearly four hundred pounds. A lot of money. We could surely get one much cheaper in England. Did he say Electrolux? 'Are you sure it's gas?'

'Oh yes. You have butane gas fittings?' No, we would have to buy two bottles, and the correct pipes and fittings. And suppose it wasn't the right size for the space occupied by the old cooker? It seemed unlikely that it would be. That would mean more woodwork before we could use it.

'How big is this cooker?' David asked cautiously. M. le Couteur consulted his catalogue again and read out the measurements. We jotted them down against the measurements we had taken before we left the boat. It seemed unlikely, a miracle even, but they corresponded exactly. We would only have to remove the old gimbals and screw the new ones into place and hang the stove onto them – not a wedge or a cut anywhere. Clearly, this was the hand of providence, this cooker was sitting waiting for *Nyala.* There was no way we could be churlish about a couple of hundred pounds one way or another.

Monsieur told us that if we took *Nyala* the four miles across the bay to Brest that afternoon he would fit the cooker and gas bottle free of charge. But what we wanted to do was to get the cooker and the gas fittings on board as quickly as possible and to get round to Douarnenez before dark. David was quite capable of fitting the cooker once we were there.

So while their van was hurtling between Brest and Camaret by road to bring the cooker to us, we were given detailed diagrams of the correct way to fit the gas pipe so as to comply with safety regulations and make sure there was no chance of the pipe wearing or fracturing, or the regulator on the gas bottle leaking at any time and filling the saloon with gas.

Because the six litre Camping Gaz butane bottle was roughly the same size and shape as the one gallon pressurised paraffin container we were discarding, we decided to put the gas bottle where the paraffin had been in the cockpit locker adjacent to the galley,

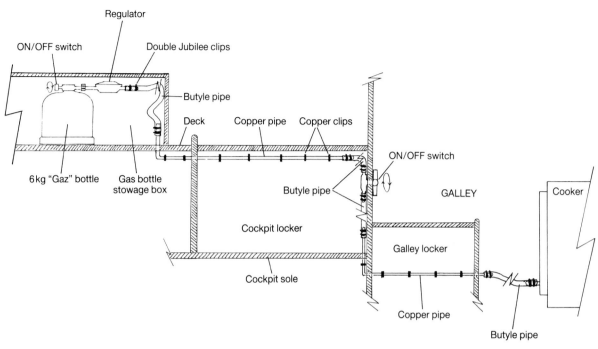

Fig 11.1 *Nyala's* final gas installation – schematic

held in place by the same ratcheted restraining strap. This meant that, to reach the cooker, the gas pipe had to pass through two bulkheads – the outer saloon bulkhead and one of the galley locker bulkheads.

Installing the feed pipe is a little tricky because it has to be flexible adjacent to the gas bottle, where it is moved around every time the bottle is changed, and also near to the cooker so that the cooker can swing freely back and forth on its gimbals. A rigid pipe in either of these situations would obviously fracture very quickly. However, where the pipe passes through solid fixed objects such as the bulkheads it has to the rigid – copper is the specified material – because if it was flexible it might chafe against the bulkheads and wear away a hole (Fig.11.1).

So it is necessary to install a 7mm pipe that is alternating butyle (of an approved standard and in date, obtainable from the butane suppliers) and copper, and to fit the two together so that there is no chance of a leak of gas at the joins. In order to achieve this the inside diameter of the butyle pipe is a fraction smaller than the outside diameter of the copper. The butyle needs to be heated in boiling water and the copper pipe greased in order to slip the former over the latter, then the join must be sealed with two stainless steel jubilee clips (being non-royalist the French call these *colliers de ser-riage*).

In a similar manner the flexible pipe is fitted to the cooker at one end and, at the other, to a regulator which controls the pressure at which the gas comes out of the cylinder. This is very critical and if the regulator is the wrong type for the appliance it just won't work.

Hanging the cooker on its new gimbals was very easy and, because the gas pipe was following the same route as the paraffin had done, there was no need even to drill holes through the bulkheads. Before the day was out we had a beautiful, shiny, three-burner-with-oven, potential bomb sitting in our galley.

I mention this uncomfortable fact because someone pointed out to us that however dangerous the leak of paraffin had been that had caused the fire, if it had been gas leaking in the same way we wouldn't have survived to tell the story. *Nyala* would have been blown out of the water as I struck the match to light the oven. As a result we have always felt uncomfortable with gas as our cooking fuel and taken precautions that have become second nature.

The first, and obvious safety factor is never to have a gas bottle installed in the saloon. Gas bottles do leak from time to time specially if they are allowed to roll and crash about, not restrained in whatever place is allocated to the spare bottles. As gas is heavier than air, every tiny bit of vapour sinks into the bilges and once a lot of these tiny leaks have collected together they make a bilge full of gas. If this does happen and you know it's there, it's possible to scoop the gas out with a bucket and throw it over the side, however silly one feels passing apparently empty buckets up through the hatches and tipping them into the sea. It's also possible to clear this gas with a bilge pump and the wise skipper generally follows the standard safety advice and pumps twenty strokes daily on a pump empty of water so as to clear any lurking gas.

Another source of gas gathering in the saloon is the cook turning on the gas tap at the cooker, then fumbling to strike a match. Most boat cookers, including ours, now have a safety valve so that it's impossible to light the gas without pressing in the knob and holding it in for several seconds after the gas had been lit. If you just turn it on and go away no gas will come out.

However, if when the cooking is finished the gas is extinguished by turning off the knob on the cooker, the pipes between the gas

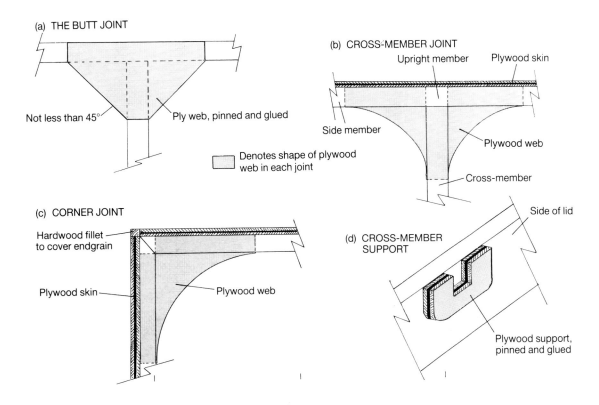

(a) THE BUTT JOINT

Not less than 45°

Ply web, pinned and glued

Denotes shape of plywood web in each joint

(b) CROSS-MEMBER JOINT

Upright member

Plywood skin

Side member

Plywood web

Cross-member

(c) CORNER JOINT

Hardwood fillet to cover endgrain

Plywood skin

Plywood web

(d) CROSS-MEMBER SUPPORT

Side of lid

Plywood support, pinned and glued

Fig 11.2 Plywood web construction – basic joints

bottle and the cooker remain full of gas and any malfunction of the knob or leak in the pipe is another potential source of danger. Again, safety recommendations are that the cooker is always turned off by shutting off the gas at the bottle first and allowing the burner to go out of its own accord before switching it off. In that way the pipe empties itself.

Since our initial hurried installation of *Nyala*'s new cooker in France, David has added the further refinements of a lockable gas bottle storage box on the afterdeck in which all the bottles – the one in use as well as the spares – stand permanently, immovably, and well out of the way. Because we were nowhere near a workbench at the time, David decided to make this box by a method of construction that would avoid complicated joints yet provide a structure strong enough to be stood or sat upon.

Borrowed from his days in wooden aircraft construction and repair, where strength is vital but the pieces are often too small and fiddly for traditional jointing, this method relies on butt joints. The strength is achieved by pinning and glueing a plywood web across the joined members (Fig.11.2). It's a useful method for the on-board carpenter because it can be adapted to make any kind of stowage lockers above or below decks, where space may be too restricted for traditional joints. The only tools needed are a mitre-box, hammer, saw and cramps, and the cutting isn't complicated.

The box was built of a 25 × 25mm iroko frame with a 12mm plywood 'skin' on the sides and ends, and curved corner pieces to hold the bottles in place. The plywood 'web' holding the joints together was provided by both the outer skin and the corner pieces that accommodated the curves of the gas bottles. The corners of the joints were mitred for neatness and the top and bottom frame pieces were supplied with 15 × 12mm rebates to accommodate the plywood outer skin (Fig 11.3).

The lid has 95 × 15mm hardwood sides and ends and, because it contains no bottle-shaped curves, the corners are strengthened with triangular hardwood butts and the cross-members with plywood location pieces (Fig.11.2).

In the assembly process the tacks hold the pieces together accurately and firmly until the glue has set but it is essential that all the right angles be true. If in doubt, cramps and corner cramps can be used to achieve symmetry. The end-grain of the plywood on the upright corners should be protected by hardwood insets. When the glue has set all the sharp edges can be rounded off with surform.

Our box is bolted through the deck, mounted on wedges under each section of frame that accommodates the curve of the deck and at the same time allow drainage space for both moisture and gas at the bottom on the outboard side. If such a box was to be mounted on a flat surface, drainage holes would have to be made at the bottom. The lid is attached with brass hinges and has hasps for padlocks.

The outer end of the copper gas supply pipe has been brought through the deck into one corner of the box and secured firmly. Attached to this is the flexible pipe which is long enough to reach any of the gas cylinders. There is an on/off tap on the regulator inside the box but David has also fitted another on/off tap in the galley bulkhead above the sink so that even in bad weather we are never tempted to use the cooker knobs to turn off the gas.

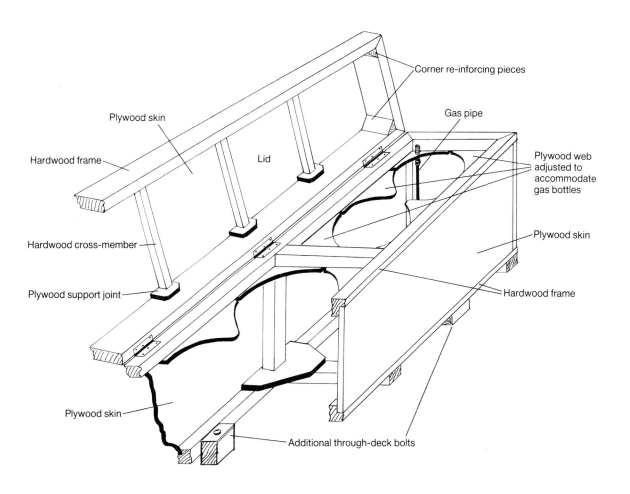

Fig 11.3 Gas bottle storage box – cut-away diagram to show method of construction

*   *   *

Under the circumstances it was quite an achievement to reach Douarnenez only a few hours late for the Festival. Although there were over a thousand boats there, some never made it at all because of the adverse weather. We were too late to claim a mooring place in the inner harbour and at first felt slightly out of things on the anchorage but as we listened to the town heaving and throbbing

137

into the early hours of the morning we realised that we were in the best place. When we wanted to join in the merriment ashore we could, yet we had grandstand seats for all the various small craft races and impromptu displays that took place in the bay.

We also found ourselves prime targets when, each afternoon, the sponsors sent a couple of fishing boats around the anchorage loaded with litre cans of Guinness and lager, which make heavy missiles, and hurled them onto the decks of all the boats, just in case anybody should become either thirsty or complacent, or think they might get away with catching up on some lost sleep. The only way to avoid serious damage to boat or to person was to catch these tins before they struck their targets and the only way to drink their contents was to leave them for a couple of hours before trying to open them.

Because we felt we were too short-handed for sailing a boat the size of *Nyala* in close-quarters situations we avoided the racing but took part in the parade of sail on the third day and, by watching closely the other boats with similar rigs to ours, we managed to solve the mystery of how to use our topsail which was on a jack-yard that had to be hoisted to the top of the mast with the sail already attached. Rather shame-facedly we struggled with the sail and the yard and the halyard and the sheet for some time before we hit on the correct combination of juxtapositioning, although we didn't feel quite so bad when we realised that the sail was still in its original folds in the sailbag; obviously nobody else had managed to sort out the system for some time before us. When we finally got it right we were so proud of ourselves, and pleased to discover that we could sail closer to the wind with the gap above the gaff boom filled.

The weather was kind for the four days of the festival, and remained so for another thirty-six hours until we'd made our way south through the Raz du Sein, which is another rock-strewn gap between the shore and an off-lying island; the French have a lot of these hazards which is probably why they are such brave sailors. Then we found ourselves in the anchorage of Audierne, together with about fifty other boats, sitting out a three-day gale from the south-east which is the only direction that bay is open to. As the breakers rolled steadily in from the Atlantic we learned that *Nyala*'s ground tackle – a 35lb CQR anchor and 45 yards of ¾ inch chain – was adequate to hold her in severe conditions on a lee shore. We also found out that, uncomfortable as we were, we could survive for three days together in a confined space without one of us wanting to push the other overboard.

When the weather moderated we pressed on southwards in heavy swell round the Pointe de Penmarch, whose winking lighthouse had been tantalising us for the last three days, and into the sheltered river estuary of Loctudy where it began to rain. All the time we had been deluding ourselves that if only we could get just a little bit further south we would find ourselves for a little while in the land of warm sunshine and be able to enjoy the rest of our cruise before setting off for home. But of course the truth is that we would have had to go almost as far south as North Africa to be out of the frontal systems that were sweeping Europe that summer. The weather was foul everywhere.

So the following day we decided to cut our losses and in heavy drizzle and a flat calm we set off back to Camaret where we would wait for the right weather conditions to make the long crossing back to Exmouth.

We reached the challenging inshore passage between the Bay of Douarnenez and the Rade de Brest, the final stretch before Camaret, after sunset. Whilst we were dodging fishing boats and finding our way through narrow passages between outcrops of rock, *Nyala*'s newly-installed navigation lights failed. The problem was a fuse which initially didn't seem very serious but every time we replaced it, it blew again. That looked bad; obviously time had to be spent tracing whatever fault in the wiring was causing the overload. Fortunately we still carried the old paraffin lamps which were soon lit and installed and once again we found the anchorage of Camaret in the dark.

The following day we were embayed by another gale and, together with several other yachts bound across the English Channel, we had to wait five days until the next window appeared between the succession of gales and fogs. We set off in conditions that were still very lively and *Nyala* buried her bowsprit several times as we left the Rade de Brest and headed north back through the Chenal du Four.

Once out of the channel and in the open water the seas were spectacular but not too big because for once wind and sea were on the right direction, on our quarter. In a fresh south-westerly we made a fast crossing to Dartmouth, where we declared our new cooker to the Customs man who boarded us as soon as we had dropped anchor. We carried on to Exmouth the next day before yet anther gale and it wasn't until we were safely on our home mooring that we could begin to dry out the bedding and equipment in the forepeak that had been soaked by the seas that had come on board as we left the Rade de Brest.

*   *   *

We felt that for two middle-aged people on a more than middle-aged boat we had done quite well in conditions that had ranged from passable to horrendous. We had made some good decisions and some that were not so clever but we hadn't got ourselves into any serious difficulties and *Nyala* had looked after us through fog and fire and gales. Our cruise had shown us that we liked *Nyala* enough to live on her. And she obviously liked us because she had given us our list of final fitting-out jobs for the coming winter, which we could only ignore at our peril.

Firstly, we needed a larger engine so that *Nyala* would have a chance of making more positive way against headwinds and heavy seas. Secondly, we had to have a completely re-wired electrical system to prevent the kind of overload that had caused the navigation lights to fail. Thirdly, we wanted an electric anchor windlass because hauling up 45 metres of chain attached to nine tons of boat was clearly either going to make us extremely strong or give one of us a heart attack very soon. Next on the list came a watertight forehatch that would keep rain and waves out of our sleeping accommodation.

Then, in case the time came when we had no choice but to press on in fog, we wanted some method of identifying the position of shipping around us. We did consider buying one of the latest breed of small yacht radars but we were worried by its potential power drain and the space it would take up. In the end we opted for a Lokata 'Watchman™' Radar Detector, which senses operating radars with a selected range, sounds an alarm when a certain shield is breached, and gives precise bearings of where these radars are. By monitoring these bearings it's possible to determine whether one is on a collision course with another vessel even though it's invisible, and since most commercial vessels and large yachts carry radar these days it provides a large degree of safety.

Finally, having had the benefit of practise, we were in the frame of mind to take fire extinguishers very seriously. *Nyala* now has a galley fire blanket, a halon gas extinguisher adjacent to the saloon engine hatch for fuel fires, and three dry-powder extinguishers, in the forepeak, the saloon and the cockpit. Their expiry dates are checked every year.

Chapter 12

A New Engine

The biggest of these jobs in terms of both time and money was installing the new engine. Making decisions which will mean the expenditure of three thousand pounds or more is a heavy matter in itself and we didn't do it in a hurry.

The Volvo-Penta MD11C that had been installed in the last major refit, before *Nyala* was ours, was still in excellent condition but it had become obvious that 23hp at max rpm was insufficient. Even in a flat calm we couldn't achieve the 6 knots hull-speed intended by the original petrol-driven Parsons D4M (fitted when she was built in 1933). A further point against it was that the MD11C had no flexible mountings so all the vibrations were transmitted through the boat. Together with the relatively high noise levels of the older generation of diesels this made off-watch sleeping difficult and on-watch conversation wearing.

We were against going back to a petrol engine for two reasons – the additional electrics necessary for a petrol engine can malfunction very quickly in a salt-water environment, and the volatility of petrol is an additional fire hazard that nobody needs on a small boat.

After some detailed research we decided that our new engine would be another Volvo-Penta, the new 2003R, giving 28hp at 3,000 rpm. Several factors pointed to this being the right choice: the extra 5 hp would give us the power we needed, the new engine would be both quieter and have flexible mountings leading to less vibration, it was lighter than the old one and *Nyala* has a tendency to trim stern-heavy, and it would fit into the space available.

When we talked about this people commented that Volvo-Penta spares are very expensive and this is true, but we are convinced that in engineering you get what you pay for. The Volvo-Pentas are tough engines and easy to service, and in fact the spares situation has been cheap so far because we haven't found that we've needed to replace anything more than oil filters, and one fuel filter. And the spares do have the advantage of being available so-called 'world-wide', though I expect there are places where any marine engine spares are hard to come by. Also, exchanging Volvo for Volvo we got a very good trade-in price for our old engine which cut the capital lay-out immediately.

We knew that a new engine would mean a new propeller with a different pitch, and possibly a different length prop shaft. We sent *Nyala*'s distinctly non-standard details to several of those suppliers who offer a computer analysis and finally ordered what was recommended, plus a new stern-tube because the old one seemed to be leaking rather too much and grease was appearing between the tube and the deadwood from time to time. It would be nice to be able to report that everything else in the process was equally well planned but it didn't really happen like that.

At the end of the summer our first concern was to have *Nyala* lifted out of the water and propped up in the boatyard only a few hundred yards along the road from our house. This yard is owned by Ron Lavis and is yet another of those old-established family boat-building and repair businesses that still survive in many of the creeks and rivers of the United Kingdom. The proximity to home would make our work very much easier and while she was there *Nyala* was to be copper-sheathed below the waterline by Ron and his assistant.

This was another expensive job but we knew that if it wasn't done we would have to dry *Nyala* out to clean and anti-foul her two or three times a year once we reached warmer waters. When we first asked Ron if he could do the job he said, 'Well, it's a long time since anyone asked me, but I think I can remember how'. With his help we had the luck to buy several hundredweight of 7.5mm copper sheets at a bargain price and he soon set to work, tarring the hull with hot pitch, pasting builder's tarred roofing paper over the top of this, tarring again, then nailing the copper in place with bronze Gripfast nails – 30 kilos in all.

As soon as *Nyala* was on dry land David started on the engine job. With the assistance of the boatyard crane the old engine came out very easily, revealing an area of bilge we had never been able to see or reach before, which yielded an interesting crop of loose nuts and bolts and a few foreign coins. It also gave us the opportunity to drop and inspect the only keel-bolt that had appeared in the X-ray to be suspect. Ron Lavis examined it and told us that even in its very slightly corroded state (2 – 3 mm), being old wrought-iron it would last far longer that anything modern he could replace it with, so David quickly put it back and turned his attention to other problems that had to be tackled before the new engine went in.

The first of these was the battery installation. The two existing 70 AH batteries had been placed on a tray in the lazarette with no means of restraint other than a 1in fiddle and their leads. Their tops were exposed and although the terminals were covered with a plastic flap, anyone carelessly pushing something metal such a bucket into the lazarette could cause a spectacular firework display. The battery master-switches were in the aft starboard cockpit locker with exposed terminals in the lazarette, again just waiting for that bucket. Although this arrangement had the advantage of a short run of cable from the switches to the batteries, the locker in which they were housed could never be properly used and, possibly most important of all, the master-switches couldn't be reached from inside the saloon with the companionway hatch closed.

The second problem demanding attention was that the mild-steel, cylindrical fuel tanks, fitted beneath the cockpit lockers on each side, blocked access to the cockpit drain seacocks making them very difficult to reach to turn on and off and impossible to service. Sorting this out would mean removing and slightly relocating the fuel tanks and while they were out it seemed like a good idea to give them a servicing and a fresh coat of paint.

As soon as David began to remove the tanks there were hints of further problems. The almost inaccessible bolts holding the tank straps in place were corroded and when the tanks were finally out – not easy since they only just fitted over the engine bearers – we saw that they were both badly corroded, both along the top and where the filler pipes joined the tanks, leaking slightly in several places. Obviously *Nyala* also needed new fuel tanks, in which case they might as well be properly designed to make maximum use of the space available and increase the fuel capacity.

And while we were about it, new fuel filters made sense – the ancient filter/separators of unknown make containing snake-like filter elements were difficult to clean and it was also impossible to see whether there was any water in them other than by opening the drain valve which was almost out of reach. David decided to replace these with Lucas 296 filters with their renewable cartridges and transparent bowls for water detection.

The old batteries and wiring came out with no problems, as did the propeller and shaft because David had the foresight to drop off the rudder when the boat was in slings coming out of the water. The stern tube came out far too easily because it was loose in its hole and the only thing keeping the water at bay was a liberal coating of grease on the outside. Investigation showed pin-hole corrosion over about 50% of the surface. The enlargement of the hole in the dead-wood was because the bolts holding the aft end of the engine bearers to the frames were found to be worn half way through, allowing the bearers to move about half a centimetre which was obviously more than the coupling had been designed to take.

This seemed a good time for the old leaking, tailor-made baffle box from the exhaust system – the one David had repaired at the start of the season – to be replaced, so it was taken round to our friend the stainless-steel welder who made a a new one exactly the same shape.

Two other modifications suggested themselves during this stripping-down period. The first was to move the stern-tube greaser which was located just inside one of the lazarette hatches and made it very difficult to stow anything in that side of the locker. The other was to rectify the lack of good bilge pumps – when we took her over *Nyala* had one submersible electric pump of unknown capacity and her original up and down pump with no strum box, operated from a very exposed position on the side deck. As we now had a lot of bilge exposed we decided to add a Henderson double-acting hand pump of 136 litres-per-minute capacity with two well-separated strum boxes, operated from inside the saloon, and replace the electric pump with a new one of 6,600 litres-per-hour capacity and a float switch. The original outside pump, which would be our last line of defence, was serviced; the old lead piping was replaced with new reinforced plastic and a strum box added.

At this stage in the proceedings David was faced with an empty and interesting-shaped but finite hole in which he had to arrange the following: 1 engine plus prop shaft and coupling, and exhaust system; 1 stern tube greaser; 3 batteries plus associated wiring; 2 fuel tanks plus filters and associated piping; 2 pumps and their associated tubes and strum boxes; piping for three cockpit drains one of which also drained the galley sink.

Not only did it seem logical to install as much as possible before the new engine was in place, it was obvious that the fuel tanks, the pumps and the cockpit drains must be done in advance. The batteries would be removable whether the engine was there or not but they needed a box to house them safely and this would be easier to fit in an empty space.

The first thing David gave his attention to was the new fuel tanks. At first he thought that ready-made rigid semi-transparent plastic tanks would be ideal but he soon found that, although these are manufactured in various combinations of boat-shape, none of them remotely matched the inside of our hull and that at best these would reduce our capacity rather than enlarge it when replacing the cylindrical tanks. Before long he had decided that we were going to have to spend the extra money involved and have tanks specially made in stainless steel to fill the space we had available.

A telephone call confirmed that one supplier would be happy to make up tanks to our specification providing we could supply adequate drawings.

The problems of producing an accurate drawing were solved by

The new fuel tanks – plywood mock-up beside a completed aluminium tank

making a wood and hardboard mock-up more or less in situ and then taking it home and measuring it up. It sounds easy but of course it wasn't. First of all, a tank that would fully utilise the space couldn't be manoeuvred over the engine bearers to get it in and out; then having made it to the size that would do this easily David found that it was just too big to go through the hatch into the engine compartment. After several more attempts he arrived at what seemed to be the optimum shape and size, one that even gave access to those cockpit-drain seacocks. But when he was drafting the final drawings he realised that he hadn't taken into account the filler, outlet, or engine-return pipes, so it was back down the road to the boatyard with the mock-up balanced on his bicycle to find the ideal positions for these.

He finally sent the drawings off one Monday afternoon and at 0900 on the Wednesday they telephoned with a verbal estimate. Then the person on the telephone asked David if he really wanted stainless steel when aluminium tanks would be lighter, cheaper and less susceptible to condensation. Knowing how quickly aluminium could corrode, David was doubtful. Then the man said, 'We make all the fuel tanks for the R.N.L.I. and they're using aluminium now. They seem very happy with it.'

That settled it. Anything that was good enough for the Lifeboat

Service was good enough for us and this advice cut the cost by almost a third. They promised a fourteen-day delivery after receiving written confirmation of the order. In fact the tanks arrived thirteen days later. What they couldn't guarantee was the length of time necessary for stove-enamelling, which they recommended, because it was sub-contracted. So we took delivery of the tanks in bare metal which David then protected by treating them with aluminium two-part etch primer followed by two coats of two-part polyurethane paint with a suitable undercoat.

The tanks fitted perfectly, fixed in place with the stainless steel straps which were lined with strips of the rubbery material that is used for anode gaskets to prevent the paint chipping and electro-lytic degeneration taking place.

Then came the installation of the fuel piping and the filters. In the old lay-out the pipes were impossible to reach other than by stand-ing on your head through the hatch in the cockpit sole. David was determined to improve on this. Removing the cockpit-sole hatch in heavy weather could be difficult and potentially dangerous, so all the fuel cut-off taps and filters would be visible and accessible from inside the saloon. The filters, one for each tank, were mounted side by side with the tops below the bottom of the fuel tanks so that they were at the lowest point in the system. This has ensured that any water in the system will remain in the filter bowl and not circulate elsewhere (Fig. 12.1).

At first David had trouble finding a source of supply of the copper tubes with all the necessary fittings, including taps, for the fuel system. Various engineering suppliers and plumbers only seemed to have half of what was required. Then Ron Lavis advised going to the local Calor Gas supplier, where everything was readily available in the correct sizes.

Because he wanted to avoid too many joins which would lead to potential leaks in the system, David bent the copper pipe around corners rather than using elbow-joints. It isn't easy to do this without flattening the pipe which restricts or cuts off the flow of the fuels. Regular plumbers use pipe-benders but we didn't have any of these so the bends were achieved by annealing the pipe.

The basic process of annealing is to heat the metal red hot then to let it cool, either at its own rate or by quenching it in cold water. This results in the copper being soft enough to bend without damage. After heating it will re-harden slowly if left to itself, when being worked it will re-harden much more quickly and copper that has work-hardened before the job is finished has to be re-annealed before continuing or it will break.

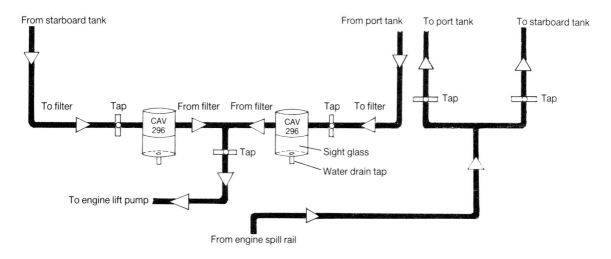

Fig 12.1 Diagram of fuel system

It was essential that these copper fuel lines be secured in such a way that the pipes wouldn't vibrate. Any vibration quickly work-hardens the copper and as it continues the pipes will fracture. All the copper piping was secured at least every six inches with copper clips lined with the soft anode-gasket material to combat chafe.

These copper clips had to be specially manufactured. Although we could have bought any amount of plastic cable and pipe clips, we discovered that it was difficult to buy copper ones in small quantities so David began to make his own. This turned out to be a good way to use up some of the off-cuts of copper from the sheathing job.

The first step was to make a jig consisting of a base plate and a pipe the size and shape of the pipe or cable to be accommodated. The base plate could be made from any piece of scrap brass, copper or tin-plate sheet that was thick enough not to bend before the copper sheet that was being shaped around it. The pipe-shaped piece was made from copper tube or brass rod of the same or slightly smaller diameter than the pipe that the clip was being made for. The two pieces, baseplate and pipe, were then soldered together and, where necessary, the joining edge was filed to a smooth contour (Fig. 12.2).

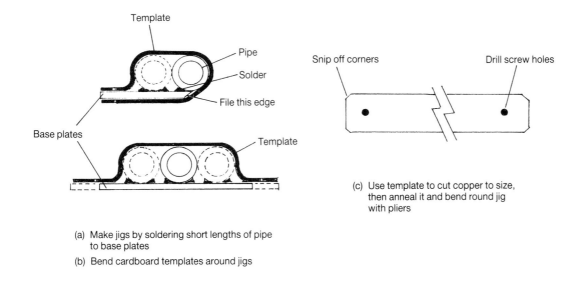

(a) Make jigs by soldering short lengths of pipe to base plates

(b) Bend cardboard templates around jigs

(c) Use template to cut copper to size, then anneal it and bend round jig with pliers

Fig 12.2 Making copper pipe and cable clips

David then made templates for the size of copper to cut for each size of clip by bending a piece of thin cardboard round the jig, marking it appropriately, then removing it and cutting it out. Placing this template on the copper sheet he marked out as many clip shapes as he required using a sharp scriber with a set square and steel rule. Then he marked the locations of the screw holes for fixing the clips, centre punched these holes and drilled them out. He then cut out each blank with tin shears. He soon found that it paid to snip off the square corners of each piece because they were sharp enough to deliver some painful scratches and the finished clips looked tidier that way anyway (Fig. 12.2).

After that each piece had to be annealed over one of the burners of the brand new Italian gas cooker, cooled by dunking in an old saucepan, then bent round the jig with the aid of a pair of pliers. Then they were ready for use. Although this process sounds complicated David soon had it down to a fine art and he found it worth the initial trouble of making the jigs to be able to produce clips to any size and shape as and when he wanted them.

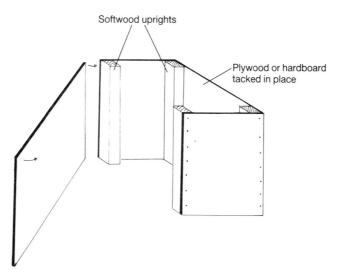

Softwood uprights

Plywood or hardboard
tacked in place

Fig 12.3 Mock-up of battery for positioning in engine arrangement

Whilst there was little choice as to the positioning of the engine
and the fuel tanks, the batteries could be accommodated in various
configurations and positions in the space to the rear of the engine
compartment. The three important factors were security, ease of
access, and not interfering with anything else. To find the best location David used plywood mock-ups – hardboard would have done
but the plywood happened to be there (Fig. 12.3). It's much easier to
juggle around three very light boxes than to hump batteries about,
and so much safer than relying on drawings and measurements
which tend to overlook such things as that bolt-head protruding
from a frame or beam. If there's something that will foul the batteries, the mock-up will find it first time.

Once the final position was decided the battery compartment was
constructed using iroko frames and 12mm marine ply, bearing in
mind that in heavy weather the nominal weight of 69 kgs would, at
a modest 1.5 G, rise to 103 kgs. As these new batteries are sealed
units they are tucked up under the cockpit deck beams which effectively prevents upwards movement but still provides a well-ventilated space.

Only after all this preliminary work had been done did David
come to the most important part of the preparations, modifying the

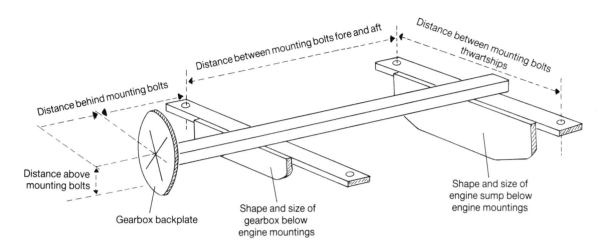

Fig 12.4 Template of engine giving position of mounting bolts, gear box backplate and other projections below mounting level

The engine compartment showing engine bearers and mountings, also cockpit drain pipes in place.

engine bearers to take the new engine. He made yet another mock-up, a full-size, three-dimensional wooden template of the underside of the engine which showed the position of each of the four mountings, and the gear-box back plate, carefully centred to pick up the prop-shaft flange, and the width and depth of the engine and gear box below engine-bearer level (Fig. 12.4). This template had to be accurate and its dimensions were taken from the Volvo-Penta sales brochure and the new engine itself, which by that time was sitting in our garden shed.

This mock-up soon revealed that, while the bearer width was the same for both engines, on the old engine the prop shaft had been approximately 2.5cm below the engine mounts, while on the new engine it was almost 2.5cm above. This meant cutting the existing bearers down by almost 5cm. Fortunately there was sufficient depth of timber to allow this to be done, although to be on the safe side David reinforced the timber bearers with 1cm thick mild steel plate at their weakest point where they were cut away to fit over a frame.

It would have been a simple job to re-shape and reinforce the bearers if they had been on a bench but working in the cramped depths of the engine compartment it took some time and cost some pain. In retrospect it would have been quicker to take out the old bearers completely and install new ones.

At last the template fitted the bearers and lined up correctly with the prop shaft. The bilge, which would probably not be revealed to the human eye again for many a year, was given the honour of a couple of coats of fresh paint then the cockpit drain pipes, the new bilge-pump strum boxes and the exhaust system were put in their places and the hole was finally declared ready to receive the new engine. As this shiny new miracle of marine engineering swung on the end of the boatyard crane one spring morning, inching down towards the cockpit, David's heart was in his mouth. Had he got it right? Was it really going to fit? Was there something vital that had been overlooked?

Mercifully, that was one part of the operation that did go according to plan. Crane-driver, boatyard workers and both of us heaved a collective sigh of pride and relief as it settled neatly and sweetly onto its bearer bolts, a perfect fit. On examination it was only two degrees out of true alignment, accurately measured with a modified protractor; minor adjustments to the height of the mountings, each fitted with an individual screw thread for this purpose, would soon take care of that.

Once the engine was in the hole David's familiar working space was restricted and he found that he had to sit astride the engine to reach each mounting in order to true up the shaft alignment perfectly. But as soon as he got it apparently right and took his weight off the engine it went out of true again; the mounts were so soft that it only required a gentle pressure to make a big difference to the alignment.

It was obvious that with the engine running under various torque loads the alignment would vary considerably, straining the shaft and the stern gear. The old, so-called flexible, coupling was going to be far too stiff for this new rubber-mounted engine. There was no way to avoid the conclusion that a replacement coupling had to be found.

Curiously, the solution was sitting on the kitchen table in the next morning's mail. In a brochure that had arrived in response to a query about noise insulation material, we found details of the 'Aqua-Drive™' flexible coupling system, which will absorb a misalignment of up to sixteen degrees out of true. The advantage of the system is that the outer end of the unit, joining the prop shaft, is bolted to a transverse bulkhead so that the propeller drives the boat directly through this bulkhead and not through the engine and its mountings. This also prevents any lateral movement of the prop shaft (Fig. 12.5).

Swallowing hard at the cost, repeating the one about the ha'p'orth of tar, David phoned an order through and the unit was delivered the following day, together with a box of insulation sheets for the engine hatches. *Nyala* being a wooden boat, it was quite a straightforward job to build the small transverse bulkhead out of iroko, fix it in place with bronze coach screws against the adjacent frame and engine bearers. The whole arrangement has worked perfectly.

Meanwhile, on the afternoon between the ordering and the arrival of the Aqua-Drive, David coupled up the fuel system and decided to fill the new fuel tanks ten litres at a time in order to calibrate the dipstick. The tanks were such a strange shape that even the manufacturers hadn't been able to predict their true capacity. It was gratifying to find out that each tank held 83 litres, enough in total for 500 miles of motoring – not that we like motoring but it is a useful safety margin.

Then, on impulse, David thought he would see how easy it would be to bleed the system through, including the engine. The Volvo 2003R is described as self-bleeding and it was very easy indeed, it only took a few moments with one bleed screw open to manually pump the fuel through.

Not long afterwards we remarked that the smell of diesel seemed

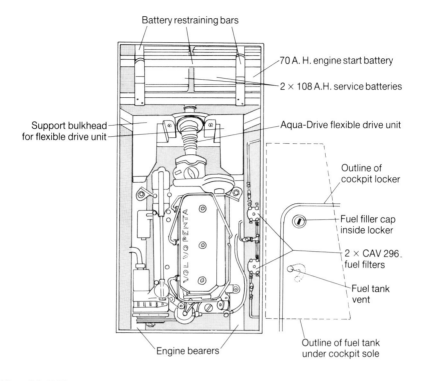

Battery restraining bars

70 A. H. engine start battery

2 × 108 A.H. service batteries

Aqua-Drive flexible drive unit

Support bulkhead
for flexible drive unit

Outline of
cockpit locker

Fuel filler cap
inside locker

2 × CAV 296
fuel filters

Fuel tank
vent

Engine bearers

Outline of fuel tank
under cockpit sole

Fig. 12.5 The engine compartment, looking through access hatch

to be increasing rather than receding. A quick examination of the bilges revealed the reason, at least ten litres had gathered in the newly painted space beneath the engine. The one pipe in the fuel system that hadn't yet been connected was the engine spill rail to the return pipe because one connecting piece was missing. David hadn't thought this would matter until the engine was running but he had carefully designed the fuel system to run on gravity alone so that it would still work in the event of fuel lift-pump failure and in this he had been totally successful. Under gravity, the fuel was steadily trickling from the spill rail.

It made a terrible mess and took some time to clear up. As a matter of interest we managed to remove the spilled diesel with the little hand pump we had bought for removing old oil from the engine when doing an oil change. To get rid of the wasted fuel, which was by that time heavily contaminated by the partially dissolved paint, we took it to our local Council tip which had facilities for disposing of used oil.

There still remained a great many finishing-off jobs, in addition to that spill-rail connection in the fuel system. There was the wiring from the alternator to the batteries and from the batteries to the master-switches, now sited just inside the companionway. There was the connection of the bilge pumps to their pipes once it became obvious which was the best way to route them around the engine – David said that for some days he felt as though he was wrestling with a demented octopus waving its tentacles from the bilges.

Then there was the throttle gear control linkage which gave very little clue as to which way round was reverse or forward, and which of course David got wrong the first time but, being aware of the possibility, he tested and corrected it before he actually had to drive the boat. There was the new stern tube with its greaser apparatus which was re-located beneath the companionway steps next to the raw water intake filter, so that we couldn't forget to give it attention.

There was the fitting of the new propeller which required sawing the new stainless-steel shaft to the required length, then drilling a hole through it for the split-pin for the prop retaining nut. This was no quick job – you can buy special drills which go through stainless-steel as quickly as normal ones go through mild steel but we didn't know that at the time. And there were the raw water intake and exhaust outlet pipes to be connected to the engine, and the electrical harness and stop cable to be fitted to the control panel.

Yes, we did wonder whether it would ever end. David was becoming more and more accustomed to moving around in the cramped spaces of the engine compartment but still every sudden move caused a lump on his head or took some more skin off his shins, and sometimes when he came home he was such a strange, hunched shape that I wondered if I was going to have to send him to an osteopath to be straightened out again.

But one happy day it was all in place (Fig. 12.5) and it was time for a trial run with a bucket of salt water to feed the cooling system. The engine started first time and all systems worked. Of course, we never expected anything else but it was a relief just the same. A week or so later, when *Nyala* had been craned into the water and were preparing to leave the boat-yard wall, I stood on the foredeck waiting to cast off the warps and wondered why David hadn't started the engine. I called, 'Is there a problem?'

'None at all,' smiled David. 'Cast off.'

The new engine in place

I did as I was told and was amazed to feel a sudden surge of power as David engaged forward gear and *Nyala* slid away from the wall. The engine had already been ticking over and, accustomed to the shattering thump-thump of the old one, I hadn't been able to hear it.

155

Chapter 13

Keeping Our Cool

It wasn't one of the things that *Nyala* recommended but it seemed a sensible idea, once we were already changing so much, that we install a fridge.

'You can't go into the tropics without any way to cool your beer,' said our Australian friend and David had to agree with him. My priorities were slightly different, I was thinking of the problems we would have keeping butter and cheese and milk usable; provided, of course, that we were in places where we could buy all these things.

Some previous owner of *Nyala* had obviously thought along the same lines because when we bought her she was fitted with a small top-loading gas fridge which was well past its prime. We were entranced with neither its murky interior and ill-fitting lid, nor the gas bottle which supplied it from a position just inside one of the main galley lockers. It just had to go. We needed that locker space rather more urgently for storing tinned and dried food and we had already decided on no gas bottles inside the saloon.

We weren't against having a gas fridge with a safer installation but we were far more interested in one of the many models that can be run off either electricity or gas and we wanted something that would take up less space. But with everything we looked at we came up against the problem that in order to fit both fridge and works into one of *Nyala*'s lockers, we would have to make some major altera-tion or another to the galley.

We had almost resigned ourselves to doing this when we came upon the Isotherm range. This seemed to provide a neat solution to our problems. It had motor, condenser, electronic sensors and cooling plate all provided as separate pieces, attached to each other by wires and a copper tube for the cooling agent. We could decide where we wanted to locate each unit, restricted only by the lengths of the wires and tubing, and build our own insulated interior for which-ever locker we thought would make the best fridge without needing to put the motor or condenser immediately adjacent. True, it was run entirely on 12 volt DC electricity but as it had a battery-state sensor that would prevent it continuing to work if the batteries were below a certain charge we thought the new electrical system David was plan-ning would be able to cope with it. We would install two small solar panels that would be continually topping up the batteries and should be able to meet the demands of the fridge. If they didn't manage this we could always run the engine for an hour or so.

After a lot of deliberation we decided to build the storage part of the fridge in the smallest of the three lockers behind the sink and cooker – for which I had already made the traditional-style doors. This would provide adequate space with the smallest Isotherm unit.

We needed to construct a solid storage box a minimum of 5 centimetres smaller all round than the inside of the locker, and we decided to make this out of fibreglass so that the interior could be lined with Gelcoat and the finish would be easy to wipe clean. To make a fibreglass shell one first needs a mould and because the locker in question was rather less rectangular than more, with a frame and a deck beam intruding into the space, the mould had to be accurate. After measuring up David constructed out of plywood and battens a male mould – i.e. the inside of the fridge compartment would be made around the outside of the mould. We were also going to need a mould for an insulating interior for the locker door, to 'plug' into the opening and for this David made a female mould but it was a smaller and more regular shape and far less trouble (Fig. 13.1).

It was then that we made our first basic error. As he was by that time very busy with the engine and the wiring, I offered to do the next part of the job. At the time I had no experience at all of working with fibreglass, other than the occasional quick repair job on our ageing Wayfarer dinghy, but David is quite an expert – he's even been on courses to learn about using the stuff – so I thought that I would be able to manage under his close supervision.

Fortunately, by that time we had a room in our house dedicated as an indoor workshop because in the English climate it's very difficult to come by suitable conditions of humidity and temperature for working with resins out of doors. The required conditions do vary from one product to another. They are always contained in the accompanying instructions and should be very carefully adhered to.

The first thing I was told to do was make the moulds as smooth as possible by filling and rubbing down the surfaces as many times as it took to eliminate the grain of the plywood and the joins of the beading. This meant a good many more times than I had allowed for but eventually we came to a compromise agreement about just how smooth the mould needed to be, and I then covered it with metallic spray paint, to provide a non-porous surface, and several coats of a special releasing agent to prevent the gelcoat sticking to the mould – if it's difficult to obtain the purpose-made product a silicone-based furniture polish does the same job very effectively.

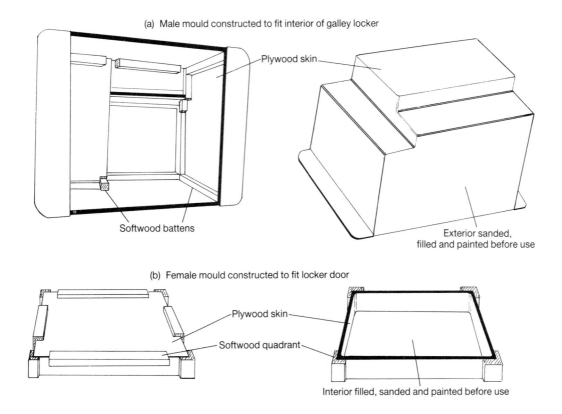

(a) Male mould constructed to fit interior of galley locker

Plywood skin

Softwood battens

Exterior sanded, filled and painted before use

(b) Female mould constructed to fit locker door

Plywood skin

Softwood quadrant

Interior filled, sanded and painted before use

Fig 13.1 Wooden moulds for fibreglass 'fridge interior

After that I had to apply a layer of two-part white Gelcoat to a thickness of about 2 millimetres, keeping the thickness as even as possible all over – not an easy thing to do with a substance of a rubbery consistency that wants to dry before you've finished spreading it. After allowing this coat time to set, I had to apply the first of several layers of fibreglass matting bonded together with two part epoxy resin. The pieces of the matting were cut small enough to bend easily around the corners of the mould but not so small that there were too many places where they overlapped, which would have made the thickness too uneven.

Fibreglass depends for its strength on this matting rather than the resin, which is only there to hold the layers of matting together, so it's important to make sure that the glass matting is thoroughly soaked in the resin, that there are no areas of resin without glass matting, and that there are no air bubbles trapped under the layers of matting.

To begin with this was quite easy but as I progressed and the resin – which only has a twenty minute working time at best – began to set bits of glass matting began to detach themselves from the fraying edges of their parent pieces and cling lovingly to the fingers of my rubber gloves and collect in bunches around the brush I was using for the resin. I began to feel as though I was the sorcerer's apprentice in some mad science-fiction movie.

To add to my anguish, David couldn't understand why I was having problems. In the usual manner of experts, he couldn't see why I couldn't simply brush the resin over the glass, a layer at a time, smoothly and evenly.

After a tense twenty-four hours, which our marriage fortunately survived, he looked at the finished job and said yes, it would do, but I'd have to sand down one or two areas of severe bubbling and apply another layer of glass and resin.

I retorted that this was a fridge, not the hull of a boat, but I did as I was told and by the following day had a better-looking job. All I had to do now was shake the mould out of the fibreglass shell and the interior of the fridge would be ready for installation.

At this point a quiet snicker or even a hollow laugh would be in order from anyone who has tried this before me. I shook the thing, then I flexed it, then I banged it gently, then very hard indeed, but the shell wouldn't budge from the mould.

I found David and told him what was happening, or rather not happening and asked him what I should try next. 'I thought that slimy stuff I put over the mould was supposed to make the two just pop apart,' I said.

With a slightly worried look on his face he agreed that yes, it was. 'How did you apply it?' he asked.

'Thick.'

'Perhaps it wasn't even enough, or perhaps you let it dry before you put the gelcoat on.'

'Perhaps,' I seethed. 'But it's a bit late to suggest that now. If it was that critical you should have told me at the time. What I want to know is, what do I do now?'

His reply was unfriendly so I went back and tried more banging, then tried sliding a carving knife between the mould and the shell which did begin to loosen it up but which also located some patches that were irrevocably bonded. Finally I ripped the mould apart, inch by inch, which was possible because it was made of plywood just pinned together, but how much easier it would have been if the mould had been constructed to take to pieces in the first place!

Instead of a shell with a nice, smooth interior I now had one with several areas of pitting in the gelcoat, so I had to fair these with Plastic Padding's 'Rust Hole Filler', which is a glass fibre paste and is a useful patching material. Then, after a lot of sandpapering, when the surface was at last looking like the interior of a fridge, I painted on several coats of white two-part gelcoat.

I had not the slightest trouble in detaching the shell for the door insulation from its female mould, so I must have done something right.

Anyone trying to work with glass fibre for the first time should be aware that some of the chemicals involved are none too user-friendly. The glass fibres themselves, although they will penetrate the skin and cause itching, are harmless but the fumes and the dust from sanding are dangerous. The first safety factor is always to work in a well-ventilated space and, unless you have a skin like a rhinoceros, wear rubber gloves. For big lay-ups and long exposure to the conditions, full protective clothing, industrial fans and venti-lating masks are essential but on a small job a throw-away plastic nose and mouth mask, overalls and a through draught will be ade-quate.

The manufacturers of fibreglass products provide special hand cleaning agents but, lacking these, a wash in warm soapy water before the resin sets will remove it from the skin. Unfortunately, to prevent the glass fibres that have lodged in overalls from penetrat-ing the skin it's best to close the pores quickly by washing in cold water. Thus the operator has to take the choice between being stuck up or needled for some time after the job has been finished.

We really thought that the worst of the job was over by then but we had reckoned without the insulation recommended by the manufacturers of the fridge unit. In fact what we now had to accom-plish was, in my opinion, almost totally impossible. We had to attach the cooling plate to the inside of the top of the fridge interior, then pass the cooling-fluid tube and the thermo-stat sensor wire through their holes adjacent to the plate, leading through the space to be insulated, through a locker, and down towards the place where we had decided to install the motor and the condenser beneath the companionway steps. All this had to be ready to push quickly into the locker and screwed in place because the insulation

The finished 'fridge in use – showing cooling plate, fibreglass interior and insulated door

material was an aerosol of expanding foam which set within twenty seconds of being released from the can. There would obviously not be much time to secure everything once the foam began to expand, with no second chances.

To get the feel of the thing we did the door insulation first. I checked that the fibreglass door 'plug' shell fitted exactly into the opening of the main fridge interior, eased it a little and sanded smooth the edge to be screwed to the door. Then I filled this shell up with the nasty-looking yellow foam that emerged from the aerosol can and, when it had dried, levelled it off and screwed it onto the inside of the door. Easy.

Having checked that the fridge shell would fit into the locker, we drilled the screw holes in the lip that would screw around the frame of the locker, then screwed the cool plate to the inside top of the shell and somehow eased two metres of delicate copper tubing down the back of the locker, through a hole in its floor and through the locker below it. Then we placed the shell almost into the locker, leaving a small gap at the top through which to poke the extended squirter tube supplied with the aerosol; we figured that before it set the expanding foam would ooze downwards rather than up.

It did. It oozed all around the fridge shell, all through the space between the shell and the locker, down through every tiny gap in the locker floor and into the adjacent locker, into the fridge interior through the holes for the cooling-fluid tube, through the edges of the adjacent bulkhead into the cockpit locker. Once we had squirted it out, we couldn't stop it from expanding and moving and we couldn't control where it was going. Nor did we have time to, because what we had to do in our twenty seconds' grace was ease the fridge interior the rest of the way into the locker and screw it into place before the foam set into too large a chunk for the space available. And of course, while we were fixing the screws the yellow foam oozed through the screw holes, through the gap around the edge of the shell, all over the screwdriver and our hands and up our sleeves.

Once the pandemonium had died down and the hard yellow crust had been scraped off everything, the rest really was easy. The motor and condenser fitted neatly into a space between the forward end of the engine bearers, just inside the saloon engine hatch beneath the companionway steps, and the electronic control unit was suspended on a copper bracket just above it. This was easy to get at and there would always be plenty of fresh air passing through the wooden grill on the cabin sole to keep the motor cool. The small switch unit was fitted on the galley bulkhead just above the sink. The wiring, following the instructions that came with the fridge, was straightforward.

Not long after we'd completed this installation job, while I was finishing the seal between the door and the fridge interior with some of that stick-on white spongy household draught excluder that is made to go around doors, it suddenly occurred to me that we could have insulated the fridge just as effectively and far more easily with blocks of polystyrene packaging. These come in quite large chunks around most new appliances and instruments one buys nowadays, and they could have been cut to size and stuck to the interior of the locker with the appropriate adhesive, thus avoiding all the mess and panic associated with the aerosol foam.

This little fridge holds far more than we expected when we

designed it and it has worked very efficiently, cooling to almost freezing point when the engine is running and keeping its contents sufficiently chilled as long as there has been enough power in the batteries.

The only design fault has been the sensitivity of the battery-state sensor, designed so that the unit will switch itself off if the battery power drops below a certain level. Because switching on the motor pulls quite a large chunk of power, this is enough to cause a temporary fall in the battery charge and unless the battery has a full charge to begin with, this starting pull takes the charge below that required to run the motor, and it switches itself off again almost immediately. The result is that, unless carefully monitored and immediately switched into its non-functioning mode, the unit will spend hours winking on and off as the battery charge scoots up and down, causing a lot of wear and not getting any cooler.

In retrospect I think we might have suffered less in the installation and experienced fewer headaches over battery state if we had opted for one of the smallest models of ready-constructed fridges. It would have meant swallowing hard, removing one of the lower, larger galley lockers and totally rebuilding it but that wouldn't have taken any longer than making the fibreglass interior for the Isotherm unit and it would have been far less painful. Just for once I feel bound to say that, although the result has been satisfactory, I think we made the wrong decision.

Fortunately it was a rare event.

Chapter 14
Getting Wired Up

It's difficult to decide which was the most challenging part of the refit, the engine installation or the electrical system. The re-engining job was big and complicated, the re-wiring was fiddly and extensive; both required patience and application beyond the normal call of DIY duty.

One of those things that every sailor learns, usually the hard way, is that electrics and water don't mix. In fact they do but the results are usually either spectacular or disastrous, or both at the same time. In theory an electrical circuit can continue to function if it is wet, provided that there is no place where the water can reach both the positive and negative wires at the same time; but because water is an excellent conducting material, as soon as it makes this bridge there will be a short circuit. In a properly fused system this will simply cause a fuse to blow; failing that it will cause overloading and possibly fire. The very least that can happen is that connecting fittings will corrode and if the water is of the salty variety this will happen all the more quickly.

In her previous refits *Nyala* had been re-wired by someone who had the advantage of a stripped out hull to work in, and he installed a system that was neat and simple and perfectly adequate to the needs of the time. However, several subsequent owners had added their own modifications by way of bits and pieces of electrical equipment by running additional wires from various junctions and the result was an overloaded switch panel and fuses.

Neither were we guiltless in this matter. Since starting work we had added a wind speed and direction indicator, a Decca navigator, a Lokata radar detector, four additional navigation lights and the Ultmar alarm system, all without making any significant alterations to the circuits or battery power. So it was hardly surprising that we found ourselves faced with that major fusing problem somewhere in the circuit that caused all our navigation lights to go on the blink whilst making our way along the French coast between Loctudy and Camaret that murky night towards the end of our cruise. If this hadn't proved too much for the installation, our decisions to install a fridge and an electric anchor windlass certainly would have done.

David's response to all this was that while we were laid up for the winter and he was doing the engine change, which involved a lot of electrical work in its own right, he would strip out all the existing wiring and do the job again from scratch. The system he designed was for 12 volt DC current running off storage batteries.

It should be remembered that the voltages mentioned here refer to western European installations – anyone reading this anywhere else in the world may have to translate the voltages according to local conditions.

We did consider whether *Nyala* should have a dual system. As more and more marinas world-wide now provide mains electricity, more small yachts are internally wired with a 240 volt AC system as well as 12 volt DC. Then, when they moor up alongside an appropriate power point they simply plug themselves in and use their 240 volt AC appliances. Large yachts, of course, can generate their own 240 volt AC supply. Although we didn't expect to be spending much time in marinas it would have been convenient just to plug into a ready-wired mains supply when it was available but David was worried by the safety implications of the difference between the two voltages.

The practical difference between AC and DC current is that, whilst AC can be more efficiently used in household appliances, it is much more expensive and difficult to generate than DC. It is also much more powerful than DC and not so forgiving when it comes to faults; anyone who gets a shock from a DC wire or faulty appliance barely feels it whereas they would be killed by AC unless they happened to be suitably insulated. Thus the wiring for AC has to be absolutely correct, with 100 per cent integrity, and appliances should be maintained in perfect order. Apart from this, supposing there was water dripping into some 240 volt AC junction box that we couldn't see, enough to make the junction box alive but not to blow the fuse? And if this damp caused a bridge between the AC and DC circuits, the DC would become AC with the potential of giving lethal shocks or causing a fire.

So we chose to stick to the safer 12 volt DC system and when we wanted to we would bring mains electricity aboard with a long heavy-duty cable and distribute it by means of an outdoor type fused 13-amp plug attached to another flex leading to a 3-pin multi-socket which enabled us to use the battery charger and anything else we wanted at the same time. The extra effort required to set this up would be minimal and because the 24 volt AC wires would always be on view we could soon see whether any of them were in a position to get wet and move them accordingly.

Having reached the conclusion that the design for *Nyala*'s system must follow the two basic principles of keeping it simple, and never putting a junction box or switch panel in a place that would be difficult to get to in an emergency, he started the job by making a list of all the equipment that had to be run off the service batteries: five navigation lights, VHF radio, Decca navigator, echo sounder, bilge pump, security alarm, wind indicator, radar detector, fridge, anchor windlass, two forepeak lights, five main saloon lights, two galley lights and two sockets to run such things as short-wave radio receiver, vacuum cleaner, fans. After that he drew a wiring diagram on paper and worked out all the loads in theory.

Fortunately David is good at physics and maths and was able to interpret the value of watts, in which all electrical appliances are rated, so that he could calculate the battery drain, size of fuse and diameter of wire needed for each appliance.

He also has a good understanding of the fundamental behaviour of electricity summarised in Ohm's Law, which states the relationship between electric current, voltage and resistance. For anyone attempting a DIY installation who feels the need to brush up on all these principles, Miner Brotherton's *The Twelve Volt Bible* is an excellent guide and reference book.

These initial calculations led to a decision to increase *Nyala*'s battery capacity to the maximum that he thought could be maintained by the engine plus two solar panels: two 108 AH coupled in parallel for services and one 70AH for engine starting. Before the electricians shake their heads and say that you can't maintain 286 AH with a 50 amp alternator – the general rule is about alternator capacity × 3 – David thought that this would work with the additional assistance of the two solar panels giving over 2 amps at midday and a double diode regulator which keeps things under control by sensing which battery has the lowest power and directing the charge only to that battery until it's full, then filling the next lowest battery. Thus, for example, when the engine is started there is a considerable drain on the 70AH battery and the regulator will make sure that battery is brought up to full charge again before allowing current into the service batteries.

Organising the theory of the system was easy enough, assembling all the necessary materials was a little more complicated and piecemeal, specially since some of the things we needed weren't readily available close to home. For example, we had to buy such apparently simple items as switch panels at the London Boat Show because it was the only place where David could make a thorough visual examination of all the alternatives before committing money to his choices. The panels he finally selected not only had more combined capacity than the old one they replaced but every switch had its own indicator light and fuse, and there was a battery-state indicator switch.

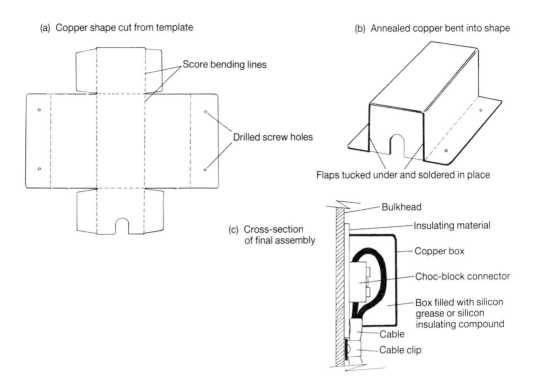

(a) Copper shape cut from template

Score bending lines

Drilled screw holes

(b) Annealed copper bent into shape

Flaps tucked under and soldered in place

(c) Cross-section of final assembly

Bulkhead

Insulating material

Copper box

Choc-block connector

Box filled with silicon grease or silicon insulating compound

Cable

Cable clip

Fig 14.1 Making a copper junction box

Some electricians would prefer to install a switch panel with trip-switches rather than fuses but changing a fuse in the fused panel is just as easy as re-setting a trip-switch. The trip-switch has several major disadvantages. The first is that it has a fixed amperage value that cannot be changed as a fuse can be, so it is sometimes necessary to wire appliances through inappropriate trips that will not respond to faulty equipment. The second is that the switch is a mechanical component which will stop working and need to be replaced if it corrodes, whereas a fuse with corroding terminals can be removed, cleaned, and continue in use. Finally, a fuse will fail safe; i.e. if the fuse corrodes it cuts off the power whereas if the trip-switch corrodes it becomes stuck in the 'on' position and is unable to respond to overload.

Copper cable clips and a junction box

Choice of junction boxes was also important. A junction box needs to have room for all its wires without overcrowding which isn't always the case in the standard plastic boxes that are available for domestic use. These are also liable to fracture and look out of place in a small boat. So in many places David manufactured his own boxes out of copper, using the same method as when making the copper cable clips but with a different template and slightly different bending procedures, and soldering the seams with a heavy-duty electric soldering iron or a gas blow-torch (Fig. 14.1).

It may not seem ideal to make a junction-box cover out of a highly conductive material such as copper but the actual wiring was done in a plastic 'choc-block' connector for the low amperage junctions; for junctions of 60 amps and over a heavy-duty metal connector was used. These connectors were then screwed to the beam or bulk-head and the copper cover screwed down over this, ideally onto a small piece of gasket material so that it would bed firmly into place and never work loose. Before the final screwing down the boxes were completely waterproofed, and the wiring insulated from the cover, by injecting them with either silicon grease or silicon insulating compound. The grease has the advantage of not setting in the same way as the compound so that it's easier to get at the junction again in the future to modify it if necessary. It should be remembered that all cables should always be led out of the bottom of any junction box so that any moisture on the cables will run away from the junction rather than settle into the box.

In every case we invested in the best equipment that was available. We bought three Vetus™ sealed batteries at what seemed at the time to be enormous expense but they have never given us a moment of trouble. In order to avoid too much voltage drop in cable runs, all cable was the heaviest duty possible for the job bearing in mind such practicalities as space available and bending the cable around corners. Because this kind of cable is expensive the runs were carefully measured before any was bought and in this context it has to be remembered that for all primary wiring, one cable run is in fact two cables, a plus and a minus polarity. All the wiring was done with red (+) and black (-) wire, the red wire always being the one to go through the switch and fuse. And remembering that a loose cable eventually becomes a fractured cable, copper clips were manufactured and used liberally as the work progressed.

The preliminary research and organisation paid off because after that the work could be dovetailed without too much interruption around the job of installing the engine. The only real hindrance was the fact that we didn't want to disturb any of the fixtures and fittings so it was quite difficult in some places to run the wires and put the connections out of sight inside lockers. In some places there was no choice but to expose the wiring to view, in which case the neatness of the job was important and was enhanced by the home made copper clips and junction boxes. In others, the job was made much easier by cultivating some very small friends who were good with their hands and managed to insert themselves into spaces that were inaccessible to either of us.

Once the place for the battery stowage had been decided and suitable restraining boxes built in the engine compartment (see Chapter 12), the work proceeded in logical order along the wiring system. First came the complete charging circuit, of 60 amp cable, which included the splitting diode supplied by Volvo-Penta for that

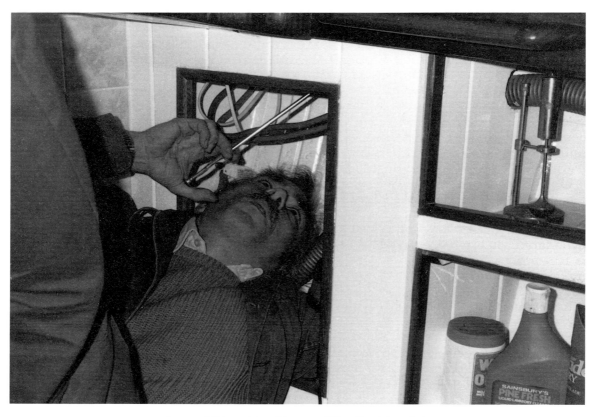

A small friend tackles a difficult wiring job

particular engine, and the master switches, available from Taplin's or Vetus, which were the simple on/off type with removable knobs rather than the multi purpose switches that are available. These switches were positioned just inside the companionway so as to be easily accessible from inside and out.

Next came the main switch panel, positioned above the chart table, with its bus bar accessible from behind through the oilskin locker. For the enlightenment of the uninitiated (like me) I should mention that a bus bar is a conducting bar that allows multiple connections to be made from one power input point. This switch panel bus bar was wired to the master switch with 60 amp cable. Then the bilge pump float switch was wired to the live side of the master switch with an in-line fuse so that it would switch itself on at any time whether the master switch was on or off.

Starting with the piece of equipment that lived nearest to the main switch panel, each of the VHF radio, Decca navigator, wind indicator, radar alarm, echo sounder, navigation table light etcetera was allocated a switch and wired up, each switch being labelled immediately it came into use. Then wires were run to the various saloon lights. The fridge, which has its own switch panel, was wired directly to the master switch. As each circuit was completed it was checked for integrity with a Multi-Tester. This useful piece of equipment for testing all kinds of values in electrical circuits is available from the suppliers of electrical components in a variety of models of different complexity.

A further run of 60 amp cable had to be installed the length of the saloon to a junction box in the heads and from this a wire (60 amp again) was run to a secondary switch panel in the forepeak which controls the forepeak lights and the navigation lights. Using this secondary switch panel cut down the numbers of wires that had to be run forward, thus avoiding unnecessary voltage drop and also saving money on the cable.

The navigation lights were wired through waterproof screw-down through-deck plugs. When we first installed these lights the previous summer I taped the wires of the port and starboard lights, which were positioned on the old wooden lightboxes, to the cap shrouds. Now, because the foresail sheets tended to chafe against these shrouds and soon wore through the tape, I encased them with French whipping in light cord. We did consider using tubes of plastic or wood to protect these wires but reckoned that these would wear against the wires as they moved, whereas now the only chafe is between the whipping and the sheets. The same principle applies to the wire for the stern light, positioned on the pushpit.

The anchor windlass consumes a lot of power when it's under load and needed a 60 amp cable all to itself. This cable was connected from the forward junction box and wired with its own master switch inside the forepeak but accessible from the outside through the fore-hatch. The main control for the windlass was a foot switch, positioned on the deck beside it but I have to say that we soon fell out with this switch which, despite being apparently waterproofed, quickly corroded and became unreliable. David replaced it with a through-deck waterproof screw-down plug similar to those used for the navigation lights, to which we could attach a press-button hand switch on the end of about a metre of cable. This cable only has to power the solenoid in the winch switch and so could be of standard 13 amp wire.

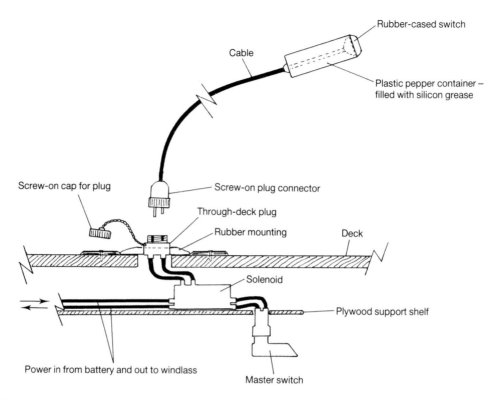

Fig 14.2 Through-deck switch arrangement for windlass, with hand-operated screw-in wanderlead

This hand switch was made from a standard waterproof spring push-button switch sealed into the top of an empty plastic pepper container, which provides something to grip whilst operating the switch and was then filled with silicon grease for insulation (Fig. 14.2). Apart from the fact that this has never broken down, it has the wonderful advantage that whoever is operating the windlass can move about freely on the foredeck, peering over the side to see where the anchor is without releasing the switch.

Although the windlass will, in theory, raise the anchor on battery power alone, the drain under load is enormous and we have made it a point never to use it without the engine running to provide immediate re-charge for the batteries.

The 12 volt sockets to run the various pieces of equipment such as the electric fans, the tape player and the vacuum cleaner – all equipment designed for car or caravan use – could be made out of continental two-pin sockets, shaver sockets or car cigarette lighter sockets. The fact that the first two of these were designed for mains electricity of 240 volts AC doesn't prevent them from being used in a 12 volt DC supply, but the same thing musn't be tried in reverse because the connections won't be strong enough.

Two solar panels providing a maximum of 3 amps were wired in parallel through a small switch panel and ammeter, located to the battery side of the services master switch. The switch panel was to provide protection for the panels if work should be necessary on the wiring between the batteries and the master switch; the ammeter was simply as a matter of interest to see how much free electricity was pouring into our batteries at any one time.

In fact it was never enough and we often kicked ourselves that we hadn't decided to install one of the several wind generators available. At the time when we were making decisions it seemed to us that such a generator would be a constant and irritating source of vibration and noise, and might at times interfere with *Nyala*'s mizzen rigging. It's true that some models of generator are intrusive but we know now that this needn't be the case, and we could easily have found somewhere to mount it out of the way if we'd set our minds to it. Boats that we've met that have wind generators almost never seem to have battery-charging problems.

Another option which we dismissed because we couldn't at that time find anyone who had tried it under serious conditions was the trailing generator, a unit that generates power by a propeller that trails over the stern of the boat. We have since learned that this works very effectively, the actual amperage available being dependent on the boat speed, but it does subtract some of the work being done by the sails towards the forward motion of the boat – in other words it slows the boat down, losing about half a knot of speed. We're not sure that it would have been wise to try out this system on *Nyala* because we measure our speed and distance run by means of a trailing log and anyone who has seen the results of a meeting between a trailing log and a fishing line will know that the prospect of the log line being eaten by the generator propeller is not a pretty one.

Initially, thinking that with a boat like *Nyala* we would be spending most of our time on anchorages, we geared up all our equipment for 12 volts, even buying a 12 volt drill and a hand sewing machine. Our first departure from this was when we met a boat carrying a Honda EK650 generator producing 220-240 volts, 650 watts AC. When we realised how comparatively light and quiet this new breed of generators is we went out and bought one for ourselves. In most boats this could live in a cockpit locker but as the access to *Nyala's* lockers is rather restricted David built a box for it bolted to the deck, just aft of the mast tabernacle (another use of the frame and web principle used to construct the gas-bottle storage box). After that we were able to re-invest in a few pieces of 240 volt AC equipment, including an electric iron which did make life on board rather more civilised. I also discovered that, because the generator has an anti-spike device which keep the supply of current steady, I could run my word-processor from it – strange as it sounds, the battery-powered lap-tops were only just coming onto the market at the time we were making our preparations.

One of the advantages of the Honda generator is that it can be used to charge the batteries. Although not as quick as using the engine when the battery power is low, it does prevent the wear on the engine that inevitably arises when using the engine without load to charge batteries. When living on a cruising boat, battery charging becomes a very important part of life and we soon learnt that keeping the batteries topped up by a small, trickling charge was much better for them, to say nothing of kinder to our tempers, than letting them run low and then having to push in a big charge quickly.

In effect we had four means of charging the batteries: the engine, which provided the big charge when necessary and always when we had to use it to move the boat; the solar panels which provided a trickle charge but were reliant on sunshine to work at their most effective rate and could keep up with the lighting but not the fridge; the generator which could keep up with most of our normal daily consumption but was better used before the power level dropped too far; mains electricity passed through a battery charger and back through the system by means of the 12 volt sockets when we are in a marina with power points – this can either provide a big boost or a trickle charge according to which way the battery charger is switched (Fig. 14.3).

We found that we had to install a circuit with an additional master-switch to cut out the splitting diode when we were charging the batteries with mains electricity through the battery-charger. For a long time we wondered why, in that situation, the batteries never seemed to be sufficiently topped up to run the fridge at its proper temperature. Finally an electrician friend suggested that the problem was that the splitting diode was never allowing the service batteries to maintain enough charge to allow the very sensitive battery-state sensor on the fridge to keep the fridge switched on. An

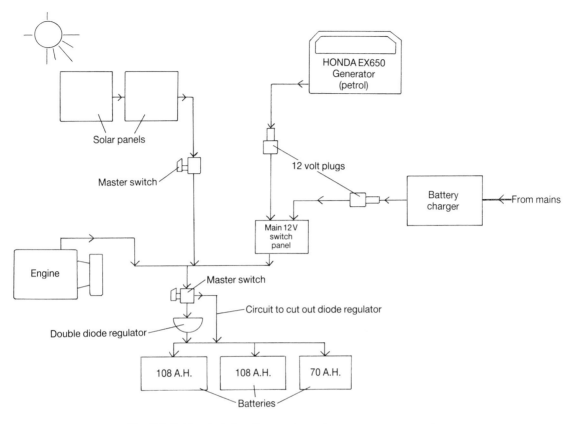

Fig 14.3 *Nyala's* battery charging arrangements

alternative solution would have been to cut out or alter the fridge's battery-state sensor but the electronic control box that governed the fridge was so much of a mystery that even the makers couldn't tell us how to adjust it.

The final important part of the electrical system is the installation of a zinc sacrificial anode – basically a lump of zinc bolted onto the outside of the hull – as an earthing system. This is necessary because in salt water an electrolytic interaction is set up between dissimilar metals which results in the basest metals wasting away. Without an anode, the electrical system will earth itself into the sea water through the propeller shaft or the skin fittings, whichever allows it the easiest path, causing corrosion. Wiring the engine block and all the through-hull fittings to the anode won't prevent this earthing process but because the zinc of the anode is the basest metal of all, that is what will wear away.

All this is explained in very clear detail in the literature issued by MG Duff Marine Limited, who manufacture zinc anodes, and David fitted an anode to *Nyala* in accordance with their instructions for a copper-clad wooden hull.

At about the time when David had sorted out *Nyala*'s electrics and explained to me how it all worked, I began to wonder whether we were really about to embark on a life that would be simpler than living in a house. After all, in our house we simply plugged every-thing into the same system, changed fuses occasionally and paid the bill every quarter. Now we were embarking on a life where we had to have sets of on/off switches between various charging systems, petrol for the generator, diesel for the engine, battery-state indicators and a steady supply of sunshine, paraffin for the back-up lamps – and we still couldn't guarantee to have cold beer or enough light to read by in the evenings.

Satisfactory though it is to be self-reliant I was beginning to learn that modern science has a lot going for it.

Chapter 15

A New Forehatch Cover

After being involved in the technicalities of installing the fridge and trying to understand what the new wiring installation was all about, returning to a bit of solid, simple carpentry was like completing a circle, arriving where I'd started from many months earlier.

There were those among our friends and self-appointed advisers who questioned the need for a new hatch cover. 'You've got a perfectly good one already – look at those beautiful strap hinges and the lovely finish that years of sanding and varnishing have given to the wood. Surely you don't want to get rid of that?'

Well, yes, after our cruise to France I did.

The trouble was that the hatch had a basic design flaw. Those beautiful strap hinges straddled a gap in the top of the hatch with a drip channel underneath that was a good idea but in practice just didn't work. It wasn't only when shipping a sea over the bows that the hatch let in water; I had only to open it with a heavy dew on the varnish for a stream of water to be rolled through the hinge opening, over the edge of the drip strip onto – you've guessed it – my share of the bunk! We tried deepening the drip channel, we had a canvas hatch-cover made but neither was really satisfactory. Something radical had to be done.

I had seen in a book, a plan by Maurice Griffiths (the designer of our boat) for a watertight hatch cover and I noticed that our lazarette hatch cover was of a far more sensible and appropriate design than the forehatch, similar to but not exactly the same as the MG design. It had a double coaming as he recommended but it lacked a water channel between the inner and outer coaming. Looking at the coaming of the existing fore-hatch hole and the space available around it, I copied the design of the lazarette hatch cover (Fig.15.1).

I used 25 × 2.5cm iroko planking which matched *Nyala*'s existing deck fittings. A piece of 15mm plywood was used to line the hatch so that it would remain completely watertight even if the top planks should shrink. Figure 15.2 shows the cutting diagram and dimensions.

I selected strong outside-mounted brass hinges and, although I could have opted for strap or toggle fastenings, for safety's sake I devised an inside/outside handle system. As nobody seems to have designed a traditional brass inside/outside handle I had to assemble my own from three separate types of fittings (Fig. 15.3) and this has worked very well.

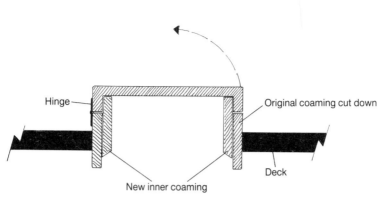

Fig 15.1 Design for new forehatch cover – cross-section

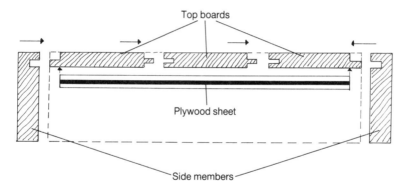

Fig 15.2 Exploded cross-section showing method of construction

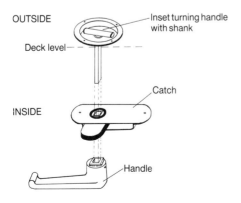

Fig 15.3 Traditional-looking outside/inside hatch handle showing assembly from three separate components

As with the adaptation of the Maurice Griffiths design and the handles, to say nothing of the use of electric tools, the method of construction was also a compromise between the traditional and the availability of modern materials. For example, if plywood hadn't been available for the hatch lining I would have had to cross-plank it, probably with pine, and without modern epoxy glue I would have been driven to using dovetail joints instead of mitres on the corners. My hatch cover is probably stronger than if I had used entirely traditional construction methods and just as pleasing to the eye.

Even though by this time I was fairly confident about all the processes I was using for this job I stuck to my rule of always trying them out first on practise off-cuts of iroko. This didn't necessarily guarantee final success but it did enable me to approach some of the work with steadier nerves.

Because my available plank was only 25cm wide I had to fit three pieces together for the main part of the cover and so the first job was to tongue-and-groove these and glue them together. As accurately as I could, I marked the tongues and grooves along the narrow edge of the timber, allowing 7.5mm width and depth and cut the grooves in the same way as I had done when making the doors.

To make the tongues I set the depth of the Proline circular electric saw to 7.5mm, clamped the board flat on the workbench and made the first cut down on each side to make a 10mm tongue. Then with the hand-plane I planed away the outside edge of this cut until I was at the required line for the tongue, again tidying up with the chisel (Fig. 15.4).

These three boards were now ready to glue together, using two-part epoxy thickened with Low-Density filler. Not forgetting to cover the workbench with clingfilm I pressed the tongues firmly into the grooves, covered with a further layer of clingfilm, then held the planks together with sash cramps. As when I was making the locker doors, I was careful not to tighten these too hard as they only needed to squeeze out the excess glue and encourage the pieces to stay together while the glue was setting. Too much pressure would produce a bow in the final piece.

Next, I cut grooves into the side pieces for the top to slot into. These grooves were 1cm deep and 1cm down from the top, made by the same method as before – I was getting pretty good at this by now and actually began to enjoy using the plough plane. I resisted the temptation to start mitreing the corners until I had the central portion ready to fit these edges to.

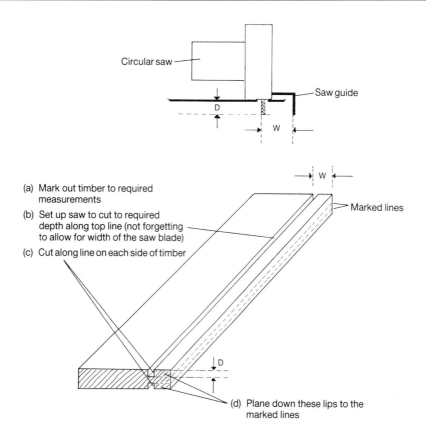

(a) Mark out timber to required measurements

(b) Set up saw to cut to required depth along top line (not forgetting to allow for width of the saw blade)

(c) Cut along line on each side of timber

(d) Plane down these lips to the marked lines

Fig 15.4 Method of cutting tongues using power saw

Once the first glueing had set I needed to trim and sand away any excess glue. At this stage I checked the measurements carefully then I marked and cut away a right angled rebate all around the top of the central piece 1cm deep and 1cm in from the edge to make the top section of the tongue that was to fit into the edging pieces. I used the Proline saw and the hand-plane, as when cutting the last set of tongues.

Next I had to glue the reinforcing plywood on the underside of this central piece. This plywood had been cut to the size required for the final hatch, less 1cm all round, so that the protruding edge of the iroko top would form the tongue to fit into the side pieces (Fig. 15.2). I didn't colour the glue for this operation as it wasn't going to

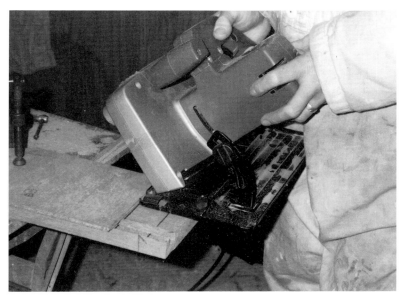

Cutting deep mitre corners with the electric circular saw

be visible. I clamped with G cramps, using spare pieces of wood as clamp pads to spread the load. It was essential that this piece of plywood should be in exactly the right place otherwise the tongue would be of varying width on different edges and wouldn't fit the grooves accurately. Therefore I had to be careful when I was clamping it as it tended to slip about while I was tightening the cramps.

Once this piece of glueing had set, the work was beginning to look like a hatch cover but I still had the most hazardous operation of all to complete, mitreing the corners of the side pieces. I have to confess that I had deliberately cut these pieces too long in the first place, to give me plenty of room for making the odd error.

For small mitreing jobs I had always used a tenon-saw with a mitre-box but this wouldn't do to cut down 11 centimetres of hardwood; I had to find another method. After several experiments I decided that the Proline saw with its fine blade set at 45% gave the cleanest cut in the hardwood, and I devised an easy method of making these cuts. First I marked the line of the cut (the inner edge of the 45%), then another line 6cm in from there. I placed a piece of thin plywood along this line and clamped the piece to be cut plus the plywood marker to the workbench. Then the blade guard of the saw could be run along the edge of the plywood giving a straight and accurate cut every time. I cut each of the eight mitres in succession, fitting each to its mate and measuring each from the last as I went along – it was the only way I could be sure of a perfect fit.

After that I thought carefully about glueing these side pieces to the centre piece. The main problem I faced was that I needed side and centre to finish up at perfect right angles to each other with all the mitres meeting exactly. Because even a millimetre of drift would have spoiled the mitres I could see no alternative to glueing all four side pieces in place at the same time, therefore I couldn't use sash cramps or bracing timbers to hold them as they don't work in two directions at once. So in order to ensure the right angles, I opted to put three screws along each side piece into the tongue. This would also give the construction additional strength though it was hardly needed; the cover was already looking like the rest of *Nyala* – strong enough to take anything the sea might throw at her.

So I drilled for the screws, locating the pilot holes in the tongue while the edge was dry of glue, and sinking 10mm holes for plugs over the tops of the screws. Then I set about the glueing, not forgetting the clingfilm on the workbench, and before the glue set I checked that all the mitres met properly and the side pieces actually did sit at right angles to the top, then put in the screws.

Once the glue had set the cover was ready for final planing and sanding. As I did this I checked that the finish was level by holding a steel straight edge across it in both directions at several points (Fig. 15.5). Then it was time to make the necessary holes for lifting ring and fastenings with brace and expansive bit. The inside-outside catches I had devised needed a 12mm hole right through the cover, and on the inside they needed 5mm pads to lift the latch clear of the surface.

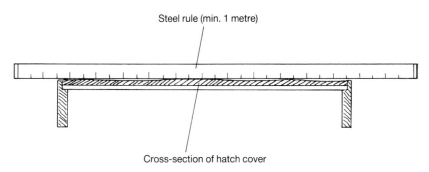

Steel rule (min. 1 metre)

Cross-section of hatch cover

Fig 15.5 Using a steel rule to check for undulations when sanding a large surface

Using adjustable drill bit to cut insets for hatch opening handles

Once all these were fixed I applied several coats of varnish, while I still had the cover indoors in a warm atmosphere.

Meanwhile, back on the boat, I needed to cut down and plane level the old hatch coaming on the foredeck. I had to remove several inches of the old coaming to lose all vestiges of the redundant drip channel and it was important that when I had finished planing, the upper edge should meet exactly with the bottom face of the new cover.

Then the new inner coaming could be fitted inside this original coaming (Fig. 15.1), first mitreing the corners by the method already described. By this time it was child's play to glue and screw this inner coaming into position. By trial and error I discovered that it couldn't protrude more than 7.5cm above the outer coaming or the hatch wouldn't open and close over it. I wish somebody had been able to tell me this vital statistic before I began as it took me some time to get it right.

Unconventionally, I had to fit the cover so that it would be forward opening because of the position of the adjacent anchor windlass and Samson post which didn't allow the necessary clearance to enable it to open sternwards. Hatches traditionally should open astern to keep things dry below if they are opened while the vessel is under-way but on a boat as small as *Nyala* it isn't necessary for anyone to use the forehatch under those circumstances, and there is plenty of ventilation from the saloon hatch which is far less likely to be engulfed by a wave or the wash of a power boat (though it has happened). In fact, the forward opening hatch has proved to be an advantage in hot climates by acting as a windscoop and providing a better through draught than would otherwise have been the case.

Once I was sure that the hatch did fit snugly on both coamings, which was only after a lot of adjustment from both inside and out, the hinges could be fitted. For security, rather than being screwed they were bolted right through the coaming and the hatch cover, and the nuts needed to be inset on the inside of the cover or it wouldn't close.

Finally I attached two sliding skylight stays to hold the hatch open when required and two small sliding barrel bolts on the inside so that it could be locked.

I was very pleased with the finished result but I soon became slightly disturbed when I was told that, in hot climates, the iroko would shrink across the grain and, because of the strength of the two-part epoxy glue I had used, the wood would then split. And the iroko would shrink at a different rate to the plywood, thus causing lifting and buckling of the top planks. Even the mitres would be likely to open in the sun. It seemed that I should have used narrower planks to minimise the effect of this shrinkage at each seam, caulked the top seams and screwed rather than glued the planks to the plywood.

But it was too late, and anyway I thought that if I'd done it the way that was being recommended, the water would have seeped in between the two layers of wood, eventually causing infuriating drips that could never have been cured.

I can report with hindsight that after three seasons of Mediterranean sun none of these terrible predictions have come true, either for my forehatch or for the lazarette hatch cover which was made before my time by the same method but of much thinner teak planks. My explanation for this is that even with the epoxy there is a great deal of flexibility in the structure, but of course when the boat is sailed and/or washed down frequently the wood is given a regular soaking which may have contributed to the planks keeping their shape.

I have had to varnish both these hatches at least once a year but this is because they are often walked on and the forehatch cover tends to tangle with the anchor and chain, and the shackles on the headsails. Eventually it became apparent that the varnished finish was a design fault anyway; when it was in good condition it was dangerously slippery underfoot and when it was in poor condition with some grip on the surface it looked bad. Because safety is more important than appearance, especially to a foredeck crew, I have recently covered it with non-slip Treadmaster™. This does slightly detract from the traditional appearance, but not much, and of course it adds extra protection from that drying sun.

We have considered that on a boat where the traditional appearance wasn't so important, the design could be varied by using a modern thick brown plastic sheet for the top of the hatch, which would allow more light into the forepeak. This plastic sheet could be set into grooves in the side pieces, mitred together as before and glued to prevent any leakage. Then modern inside/outside hatch handles could be fitted through the plastic without the need to modify the brass fittings as we had to for *Nyala*.

The forehatch finished, the engine working, the wiring completed, we both raised our heads and wondered what our next job should be. What we saw around us was the real world, already well into summer with new places crying out to be visited. Even the English Channel looks inviting in July and we were itching to be on our way so that we could find a warm climate for the coming winter. Surely after so much work we could safely declare *Nyala* fit for living and travelling on?

So what was keeping us?

The completed forehatch cover in place

Nyala's steering wheel.

Getting Away

Not a lot.

Just one more formidable hurdle: stowage.

When I say that the two of us lived in a five-bedroomed house and every room was used purposefully, cluttered with the necessities of our various professions and projects, the scale of the problem begins to emerge. We thought we'd worked out what we could take with us and what we couldn't but as we sorted and packed and discarded we still asked each other a dozen times a day, 'How are we going to manage without that?' and 'Where are we going to put it all?'

We began the process well in advance, sorting our possessions into four categories: (i) things we would need to take with us; (ii) things we were sure we didn't need or want to keep and would therefore sell or give away; (iii) things we couldn't take with us but couldn't bear to part with which would go into store; (iv) things we couldn't quite make up our minds about, would like to take with us if there was space or might sell if we could get a good enough price.

Category (i) was easy enough to define and as long as we followed the rule of deciding where we would stow it before allowing it on board we managed to keep it under control, at least in the early stages. Neither did category (ii) present many problems at first; we had never sorted out the possessions accumulated by combining our two separate households a few years previously, and by inheriting much of David's parents' household quite recently. We were rather surprised to discover that we possessed twenty-seven pairs of pliers but it wasn't hard to decide that we didn't need them all.

Category (iii) included family papers and photographs, pictures and household ornaments that had been collected over the years and could never be replaced, a few precious books, the model railway David had made. The only real problem was category (iv), which grew in direct proportion to how tired we were at the time. We knew it would be a physical strain to sort out dozens of cupboards full of personal possessions but we had no idea just how emotionally and mentally exhausting it would become when we were faced with the necessity to make a major decision about every item we held in our hands. In the end category (iv) became the repository of shelved decisions and the only thing that kept it under any sort of control was the awful knowledge that if we never got around to dealing with it, the items we had allocated to it might be lost to us for ever.

The selling we had to do took place through a series of car boot sales for the smaller items and advertisements in the local newspaper for the larger, more expensive things like furniture and household appliances. Gradually our possessions dwindled and there were more and more empty, echoing rooms. But still, with a sense of panic, we saw the date approaching when we had agreed to complete the sale of the house and it was by no means empty enough. Something drastic had to be done.

We hit upon the idea of declaring our last Sunday ashore an 'Open Day'. We passed the word around all our friends that we would be entertaining from morning coffee time throughout the day until the evening so that we could say goodbye to everyone. At the same time everything that remained unwanted in the house would be for sale at whatever prices they cared to bid and we would donate ten per cent of the proceeds to the Royal National Lifeboat Institution.

It was a memorable day. They came in scores, friends and neighbours from past and present, with wheelbarrows, vans and car trailers. They drank coffee, tea, wine, beer, consumed a mountain of sandwiches, and even those who had intended only to talk and shake our hands departed clutching something they valued that had only cost them a few pence or a pound or two. At the end of the day there was nothing left except a heap of things in boxes and plastic sacks waiting in our garden shed to be transported to *Nyala*. Even our bed had been promised to a neighbour as soon as we had slept our last night on it.

So it came, the last chance day, time to move properly on board, to declare ourselves full-time, real, liveaboard seafarers at last. Our faithful Tinker Traveller made just one more journey across the estuary, then just one more and just one more again, and as the pace increased we didn't have time to stow anything properly on *Nyala*, we just had to dump it on board and hurry back for more. By evening, after crawling on board over an afterdeck and cockpit piled high with boxes and bulging black plastic bags, we collapsed in the saloon on top of yet more boxes and bags, and stared at each other, eyes glazed.

'We've made it!'

We were bemused, exhausted and yet triumphant. We opened a bottle of Scotch that I was careful not to have buried too deeply and had a few celebratory snorts. Then we cleared the bags off the saloon bunks and fell asleep.

The next morning we couldn't even make breakfast until we had sorted and stowed some of the muddle and we looked around, appalled, wondering where to start. There was so much stuff! Where had it all come from and, for heaven's sake, where was it all to go? We thought we'd carefully planned it all but now we began to wonder if we'd made some awful error in calculating the logistics.

'Everything' included all the normal yachting gear and safety equipment, food and water, engine spares, extra sails, additional anchor chain, tools, books, music tapes and player, photographic and art materials, several different kinds of spare fuel, galley equipment, every stitch of clothing we possessed, bedding and linen, a sewing machine, the generator, the word processor . . .

We calmed our panic with reason. There must be a place for it all, it was only a question of making a start, opening one of the boxes or bags and putting its contents in a suitable place. We told ourselves we'd soon have everything shipshape.

We soon realised what a silly idea that was. The problem is that there is very little that's shipshape, except for ships. Books, utensils, boxes of first-aid equipment are all corners and straight lines while the lockers on a boat are composed of smooth, unpredictable curves with odd obstructions protruding from them – obstructions very necessary to the construction of the vessel but totally defeating to anyone trying to pack the space efficiently. The only items that will properly accommodate the odd-shaped spaces available are bags of bedding and clothing, and the sails. We soon began to wonder if there wouldn't be a big profit for the person who could design a range of equipment with two straight edges and a sort of continuous curve in place of the other two edges – truly shipshape. Or would that have been taking some of the challenge out of the whole process?

The rules about stowage on a small vessel say that the most weight should go low down and as near to the centre of effort as possible. This keeps the centre of gravity in the best place for efficient sailing. It's also important to keep the balance and trim of the boat correct. We tried to bear all this in mind but the realities dictated their own rules.

For example, however heavy an item might be, if it would be needed often it was senseless to put it close to the mast at the bottom of the forepeak locker. And something that we hoped we would never have to use at all, such as the flares or the bolt-croppers or the axe, were going to be useless in an emergency if they weren't stowed where we could put our hands on them in a matter of seconds. Then we discovered that, while it was comparatively easy to stow lots of small bits and pieces, larger items had to be found a home first because as the space diminished it was more difficult to fit them in. This led to several instances where one of us would have to unpack some locker that had just been carefully filled by the other simply because there was no other place large enough to hold the next item to be stowed.

What had seemed like useful containers suddenly became most unhelpful. The large plastic tool-tidy that had always held our stock of tobacco tins containing brass screws just wouldn't fit anywhere, except in the space allocated to the word-processor; but the tins themselves without their container finally stowed very well into one of the saloon drawers. Of course, putting them there meant finding a new place for the spare torch batteries and electrical fuses.

Tools that had lived for years in nice wood or metal boxes had to be transferred into old-fashioned tool rolls, some of which were bought second-hand at those car boot sales, others made by a nimble-fingered friend. These not only fitted more easily into lockers, they kept moisture away from metal surfaces and stopped the tools banging about in rough weather.

We found that there was a lot that could be attached to the bulkheads once we'd put up enough hooks or made appropriate handy little brackets. We also scrabbled about opening up unlikely hidey-holes underneath built-in lockers and compartments. Twenty-five metres of spare chain was snaked back and forth in the two-inch gap between the top of the port water tank and the saloon berth. The corresponding space on the starboard side held some spare sheets of copper and the volumes of the sight-reduction tables for astro-navigation.

In the end there really was a place for everything but it wasn't always easy to resist the temptation to chuck some of it over the side in desperation. There were certainly one or two things we decided that perhaps we could do without after all, but not many. Not nearly as many as the things we later found that we needed and had to find more space for.

Finally, several inches lower in the water than the day she had been launched earlier in the summer but clear of all the clutter of cardboard boxes and other unnecessaries, *Nyala* was declared ready to set sail. We were paid a succession of farewell visits by various members of our family, the same who had so visibly shuddered at their first sight of *Nyala*'s damp, smelly interior in Queen Anne's Battery nearly two years ago. Now they glanced around at the fresh paint, the varnish and the cushions and said things like, 'Isn't this cosy?'

*   *   *

David and I, just after moving on board *Nyala*. (Photo by Tim Cuff)

'When are you actually going?' asked my sister.

This was now the question uppermost in the minds of all our family. They took the water-taxi out to our mooring for a visit on every possible opportunity just in case it might be their last chance to speak to us, ever. It was also a question that was occupying us because we'd over-run by some weeks the fortnight we'd allowed ourselves to live on the Exmouth mooring while we tidied up our affairs. Summer was over, the autumn equinox approached and we would soon be short of time to find a warm place to spend the winter.

Tentatively, aware that a firm decision might well cause floods of tears from my mother, I said, 'We thought tomorrow's early tide'. We really did. The time had come at last.

My sister headed off an emotional crisis by smiling broadly.

'Right,' she said firmly. 'Let the adventure begin.'

And it did.

Nyala under sail in the Mediterranean – 1993.

Appendix 1

Useful Addresses –
by chapter in which they are first mentioned.

*(N.B. All these addresses were correct at the time of going to press.
No responsibility can be taken for any changes made since, or any omissions.)*

Chapter 1

Surveys:
The Yacht Brokers, Designers and Surveyors Association, Wheel House, Petersfield Road, Whitehall, Bordon, Hampshire GU35 9BU.
(Send on request a list of member brokers, designers and surveyors in most regions of Britain and Ireland.)

Registration:
Department of Transport, General Register and Record Office of Shipping and Seamen, Block 2, Government Buildings, St. Agnes Road, Gabalfa, Cardiff CF4 4YA (or P.O. Box 165, Gabalfa, Cardiff CF4 4UX).

Insurance:
All the following offer insurance for classic boats (i.e. those beyond the first flush of their youth). Acceptance depends on survey.

Hogg Insurance Brokers, Yacht Section, Marine Division, Insurance House, 125–129 Vaughan Way, Leicester, LE1 4SB.

Hayes Parsons Ltd., St. Lawrence House, Broad Street, Bristol, BS1 2EJ.

K.C. Powell & Partners Ltd., 50 The Broadway, Leigh-on-Sea, Essex, SS9 1AG.

Classic Marine, 648 – 656 Glasgow Road, Wishaw, Strathclyde, ML2 7SL, Scotland. (Also a range of traditional fixtures and fittings).

Haven Knox-Johnston, 134-138 Borough High Street, London, SE1 1LB.

Chapter 2

Timber & Fastenings:
Robbins Timber, Merrywood Road, Bedminster, Bristol, BS3 1DX.

Vincent Murphy & Company Ltd., 22–24 Juliet Way, Purfleet Industrial Park, Purfleet, Essex, RM15 4YD.

Milland Fine Timber Ltd., The Working Tree, Milland, Nr. Liphook, Hants, GU30 7JS.

Fastenings:
Davey & Company, 1 Chelmsford Road Industrial Estate, Great Dunmow, Essex, CM6 1HD.
(Traditional fastenings and many other things.)

Combwich Marine Enterprises, Quay House, Riverside, Combwich, Bridgwater, Somerset, TA5 2QZ.
(Specialise in silicon-bronze fastenings).

Tools:
Buck & Ryan Ltd., 101 Tottenham Court Road, London, W1P 0DY.
(It is worth sending for their illustrated catalogue just to feast your eyes on the pictures).

Adhesives:
WEST SYSTEM*, Wessex Resins & Adhesives Ltd.,189-193 Spring Road, Sholing, Southampton SO2 7NY.
(*Reg. Trade Mark).

SP Systems, Montecatini Advanced Materials, Love Lane, Cowes, Isle of Wight, PO31 7EU.

(Both the above will send full information on the use of their products.)

Chapter 3

Heaters, Flues and Chimneys:
Pumpkin Marine & Leisure, 100 The Highway, London, E1 9BX.

Cruisermart, 36-38 Eastern Esplanade, Southend-on-Sea, Essex, SS1 2ES.

London Yacht Centre, Department S3, 13 Artillery Lane, London, E1 7LP.

Shamrock Chandlery, Shamrock Quay, William Street, Northam, Southampton, SO1 1QL.

(All the above are general chandlers carrying a very comprehensive stock and operating mail order services)

Flue Cleaner:
Stovax Ltd., Falcon Road, Exeter, Devon, EX2 7LF.

2-part Putty & Filler:
The Milliput Company, Unit 5, The Marian, Dolgellau. Mid Wales, LL40 1UU.

Chapter 4

Toilets:
Blakes & Taylors, Chillington Marine Ltd., Unit 1, Newtown Business Park, Ringwood Road, Poole, Dorset, BH12 3LJ.

(Also, all the chandlers listed in Chapter 3.)

Waste, Water and Fuel tanks:
Malcolm Cole Ltd., 10 Chantry Park, Cowley Road, Nuffield Industrial Estate, Poole, Dorset, BH17 7UJ.

Rigid Plastic Tank Company, 42 Howard Road, Bedminster, Bristol, BS3 1QE.

Seaflex Limited, Samuel Whites, Cowes, Isle of Wight, PO31 7DU.

Air Cushion Ltd., Unit 6, Belgrave Road Industrial Estate, Belgrave Road, Portswood, Southampton, SO2 3EA.

Sealants:
Marine & Industrial Sealants, 8 Westwick Hill, Westwick, Norwich,
Norfolk, NR10 5BQ.

Chapter 5

Steering and Control Equipment:
Whitlock Marine Steering Co.Ltd.,Crescent House, Latimer Road, Luton,
Bedfordshire, LU1 3UZ.

Autohelm, Nautech Limited, Anchorage Park, Portsmouth, Hampshire, PO3 5TD.

Chapter 6

Tinker Inflatable/Liferaft:
Henshaw Inflatables Limited, Bennetts Field Trading Estate, Wincanton,
Somerset, BA9 9DT.

Epoxy Filler:
Plastic Padding Ltd., Woodburn Industrial Park, Woodburn Green, High Wycombe,
Bucks, HP10 0PE.

Chapter 9

Varnishes:
Blakes Marine Paints Limited, Harbour Road, Gosport, Hampshire, PO12 1BQ.

International Paint Ltd., 24-30 Canute Road, Southampton, SO9 3AS.

Chapter 10

Material, Foam and Zips:
D.B. Marine Sales Ltd.,Riverside, Bathpool, Taunton, Somerset.

Chapter 12

Engines:
Volvo-Penta, Volvo Penta UK Ltd., Otterspool Way, Watford, Herts, WD2 8HW.

Yanmar Marine Diesel Engines, E.P. Barrus Ltd., Launton Road, Bicester, Oxfordshire, OX6 0UR.

Nanni Diesel, Darglow Marine Ltd., Upton Cross, Poole, Dorset, BH16 5PH.

BMW Marine Engines, P.H. Marine, Val Wyatt Marina, Wargrave, Berks, RG10 8DY.

Fuel Installation:
CAV 'Filtrap' Fuel Filters, Lucas Automotive Limited, Windmill Road, Haddenham, Aylesbury, Bucks HP17 8JB

Aquadrive, Exhaust Silencers, Noise Insulation, Non-slip flooring:
Halyard Marine & Industrial, Whaddon Business Park, Southampton Road, Whaddon, Nr. Salisbury, SP5 3HF.

Propeller, Shaft etc;
Teignbridge Propellers Ltd., Decoy Industrial Estate, Newton Abbott, Devon ,TQ12 5NB.

Chapter 14

Batteries:
Vetus den Ouden Ltd.,Unit 38-39 Brunel Road, South Hampshire Industrial Park, Totton, Southampton, Hants, SO4 3SA.
(Also a wide variety of high quality engine, electrical and general fittings).

Electronic Components:
Maplin Electronics, P.O. Box 3, Rayleigh, Essex, SS6 8LR.

Electrical Equipment:
Taplins Marine, Unit 12, Shamrock Quay, Southampton, SO1 1QL.

Anodes:
M.G. Duff Marine Limited, Birdham, Chichester, West Sussex, PO20 7EW.

Appendix 2

Prices

N.B. It is impossible to be specific about costs, partly because one never counts every little item that is bought at the local chandler during a refit, partly because even in the short time that has elapsed since we did the work on *Nyala* prices have risen quite considerably for some items, while others are no longer available at all. This list should be taken as the roughest of guides.

THE BOAT:
There is no rule of thumb for classic boats. It depends very much on condition and how badly you want to buy that particular boat. *Nyala* cost us £17,500.

SURVEY:
The Yacht Brokers, Designers & Surveyors Association (address above) recommend the following formula which operates for their members in most of the South of England, but can vary according to distances to be travelled:
(Length × Breadth) ÷ 1.2 = £. Our total came to about £300.

INSURANCE:
Fully comprehensive including personal effects and up to £500,000 third party, £500 annually.

REGISTRATION:
Change of name on Registration Document – £47.00.

SMALL ARCTIC STOVE:
£175.

FLUE PIPE, CHIMNEY AND THROUGH-DECK FITTING:
£60

FIXING BANDS AND INTERNAL GRATE FOR STOVE:
£50

FLUE CLEANING POWDER:
£6.50 per pack

PAR/BRYDON TOILET:
£89

HAND WASHBASIN:
£2 second-hand. New stainless-steel from £27.50

'FLIPPER' WATER PUMP TAP:
from £56

HOSE:
from 95p per metre

SKIN FITTINGS:
from around £3 each

SEACOCKS, which include skin fittings:
from £56

AUTOHELM 4000:
£395 plus £37.50 for wooden wheel fixing kit

WIRE ROPE:
from 47p per metre

RADAR REFLECTOR:
Firdell 'Blipper' from £80

NAVIGATION LIGHTS:
Aqua Signal Series 41 for vessels up to 40 metres, £40 per light.

JACKSTAYS AND COCKPIT STRONG POINTS:
Wire rope and Talurit splicing – Approx £20. U-bolts from £5 each.

TINKER TRAVELLER INFLATABLE SAILING TENDER AND LIFERAFT:
£2,945

DECK LIGHTS:
from £37.50

BRASS HINGES:
from 80p according to size

DOOR CATCHES:
from £6 each

BARREL BOLTS:
from 50p each

BRASS VENTILATOR COWLS:
from £60

BRONZE MUSHROOM VENTILATORS:
from £28.75

NON-FLAMMABLE UPHOLSTERY FOAM:
78′ × 23′ × 4′ – £47

COOKER:
Can cost anything from £200 to £1,000.
Ours cost £450 with all fitting and two 6-litre bottles of Camping Gaz.

FIRE EXTINGUISHERS:
1.36 kg dry powder £27.60
Halon Gas £23.50
Fire blanket £27.00

ENGINE:
Volvo Penta 2003L – £3,144

PROPELLER:
£104

SHAFT:
£57

GREASER ASSEMBLY:
£28

STERNTUBE ASSEMBLY:
£129

FUEL TANKS AND FIXING STRAPS:
£518

AQUADRIVE UNIT with coupling clips:
£510

NOISE INSULATION:
from £70.50 for 2-sheet pack

REFRIGERATOR UNIT:
Isotherm 3000 from £640

GENERATOR:
Honda EX650 – £457

SWITCH PANELS:
4-way £11.50 – 13-way £79.50

WINDLASS:
Seawolf Electric £690

SOLENOID:
£28

FOOT SWITCH:
£22

BATTERIES:
Vetus sealed maintenance free – 70 AH £94.20 – 108 AH £107.50

TREADMASTER non-slip flooring:
from £29 per sheet

Index